# VOLUME 1

# Letters from the Stars

# MARY LADYBIRD SPIRITLIGHT

*channeled* ENCODED PROSE & POEMS

# VOLUME 1

# Letters from the Stars

## MESSAGES *for* THE NEW EARTH

# MARY LADYBIRD SPIRITLIGHT

*channeled* ENCODED PROSE & POEMS

Published by
LADYBIRD PUBLISHING
Grafton, Massachusetts 01519
www.ladybirdpublishing.com



Library of Congress Control Number:
2026905565

**ISBN:**
979-8-9951087-0-2

Illustrations and Cover design by Mary Ladybird
*(cover illustration with help from AI)*

**Printed in the USA**

# CONTENTS

# MESSAGES *for* THE NEW EARTH

## I AM THE STORYTELLER

of the new way
I am here to write a story of the new beginning
I am here to write the story in this hour
In the glory of a new heaven
Yes, you are on your way
***Do you know who you are, truly, and who you will be?***
Destiny at your door, you will see
The fire you need is coming soon
It's the fire you need to bloom
To burst out of the seed
Into a tall tree

*Nothing more to do*
*Just breathe*

The space between worlds
That's where I live and dream
In the realm of the unseen
It's time to believe in your dreams

As they say, the road is not narrow and straight
But more like a river
Making its way to the lake

Make no mistake, this road you must go
Moving fast or slow
Will lead you
Home

## PREFACE

# How it All Started

It was on a sunny morning, peacefully living in my rented condo when I opened my computer to an email from my landlord telling me I had to move out. The prices of homes were skyrocketing (late 2021) and he was jumping at the opportunity to sell the place for a huge profit. I failed to realize that divine intervention was at hand, and in hindsight, moving out was part of my path forward.

***Sometimes discomfort is the medicine we need.***

The condo, pool, and woods behind my home had become an oasis for myself and my daughter. I had just survived a traumatic divorce a few years back and the thought of packing all my belongings to find another home was devastating—definitively not what I planned.

I was determined to own a home rather than rent. I never wanted to be in a situation again where someone could kick me out. After two months of scrambling, bidding, and "losing", I finally bought my new home. This small condo was out in the country, where The Nipmuc Nation Tribe live, also known as the "Fresh Water

People." The woods were close by and I felt connected to the area and it's history.

The night I moved into my empty, echoing condo, I sat down to meditate. I welcomed the new space with ceremony, eager to transform it into my new sanctuary. I had no idea how my life, as I knew it, was about to change. What happened next, I would've never expected.

***This was when it all began.***

Sitting in meditation, sounds began to come out of me: "Ahhhhh, Eeeeeee!" I had no idea what was happening or where it was coming from. I distinctly remember saying out loud, "Interesting. I wonder if this house is going to teach me to channel."

***I believe I have moved onto sacred native land,
with portals behind my home.***

Five months later, I became a channel. It started with my handsome, but feisty, orange Maine Coon cat named Major. He began wanting to go outside every night; this was not typical for him. At the time, I didn't think much of it.

I noticed that he was going to a certain spot every night on the other side of the duplex. It was a secluded area with bushes and trees. I would go out on my balcony, that overlooks the front of the home, trying to see where Major was going.

I often went out on the balcony for fresh air and to look at the stars. I was drawn to one particular star that night, which appeared directly in-line with my balcony. I watched this star over the next several nights. One evening, I was in my living room, when I suddenly felt called to go to the balcony, so I slid open the glass door and stepped out.

Except this time, when I looked at the sky, I saw a feather-shaped cloud. After noticing the cloud, my eyes found the star I had been watching and it started to change. Suddenly, it wasn't just starlight. The light changed direction into three specific paths: one going up and two coming out diagonally on the bottom, forming a triangle, like an inner peace symbol. Every lamppost along my road turned their beams skyward, like rows of flashlights, as though the star above was pulling the light and energy upward, towards it.

I blinked my eyes to make sure I was seeing clearly, trying to adjust them to make sense of what I was witnessing. I thought to myself, "Why would the lights be changing like that?"

I looked back up at the star, but to my surprise, I saw what appeared to be a space craft; a small, twinkling light floated off from the main star. Out loud, I said,

*"They're coming! Oh my gosh, they're coming to see me!"*

I knew at that moment it hadn't been a star I had been watching but rather a galactic craft. It had also been watching me in disguise.

I immediately ran to bring Major inside and found him in the spot behind the bushes. I waited at the door, anxiously watching for signs. I couldn't see them with my physical eyes, but I felt the shift of energy around me, and knew, they had arrived at my door. I opened the door for them and said, "Welcome to my home. I am Mary. Please come in only if you are here for my highest good." Intuitively, I went to my bedroom to lay down. I could feel them following me. I laid down in my bed and said, "Do what you need to do. I am ready."

I had to have faith and trust in that moment. As I laid there, I suddenly felt a sensation on my head that felt like tingling, but from within. From what I could gather, they were using some type of laser technology. I could feel the invisible lasers, moving diagonally and across layers of my brain.

At the time, I didn't understand what they were doing. Looking back, I believe the visitors were decalcifying my pineal gland. Many people pursue decalcification for spiritual enhancement, including improved intuition and a deeper spiritual connection. Based on this experience, the Being that preformed this is known in the spiritual community as a psychic surgeon.

They *(my guess is Sirian origin...or Avaian, due to seeing the feather shape cloud earlier)* did what they needed to do and then left. There were no words. I don't have any conscious memory of experiences like this in my past. All I knew was that I had just been visited by a being from a galactic race.

Reflecting back on the situation, I now believe Major was somehow raising the vibration and clearing the space for the "craft" to land: silently and invisible to the human eye. To this day, he has no interest to visit that spot of land. I still have doubts, yet I know cats are powerful at detecting energies humans can't see. I believe that animals also have a mission— we just don't always notice it.

That evening, I was processing everything from the visitation. Naturally, I wanted to understand what had just happened. I found myself going onto YouTube, where a video caught my attention titled, *I Will Activate Your Light Language.* I was curious, as I had never heard of light language. I was entranced while watching a women speak these different sounds and move her hands in what I would call mudras. Over the next couple of days nothing seemed to happen, so I assumed the decalcifying and the Light Language activation didn't work.

Three days later, I was experiencing back pain and decided to lay on my new acupuncture mat. Trying to get comfortable, my head suddenly started moving quickly, as if I were shaking my head "no" repeatedly. I felt swept into a tunnel or wormhole, suddenly I was in outer space surrounded by stars. I was being transported on a journey from star system to star system. I felt a guardian fly with me to each star system. I was divinely lead in this beautiful journey through the stars.

Still traveling through the wormhole of star systems, I began to speak but it was not English. At first, it sounded like gibberish, but then I started speaking as if I were a bee buzzing around. Then I'd fly off to another place, speaking a different "language" each time. This went on for maybe thirty minutes. I finally got off the acupuncture mat and realized—light language had been flowing through me!

I couldn't believe it was happening! I was so excited, dumbfounded, and grateful all at the same time. I had been broken wide open...my internal antenna was suddenly getting all the galactic stations.

It took six months to understand how to harness this new gift because soon after the opening I was thrown into a spiritual crisis. My "antenna", third eye, was blown wide open. I had walk-ins, possessions, and controlling reptilian experiences. I was pushed directly into the darkest "dark night of the soul" journey I've ever been on. I needed to learn how to refine the opening, set spiritual boundaries, heal trauma, and learn to trust spirit again.

It's been an adventure getting to know this new form of channeling and how Light Language can be utilized for healing, both for myself and others.

There is much we don't see, yet we know it exists. Take something as simple as air, for example, it keeps us alive and we know it intimately, yet we've never seen it. I see this experience as being just as life-affirming and believable as the air we breathe.

Everyone's experience of Light Language is different. No, it doesn't have to be as extreme as aliens coming down to visit you. You don't need this experience to access Light Language or channeling. When the time is right, and you are ready for it, it will happen. The awakening process, yes—it is a process—started in 2016 for me and the layers continue to peel off.

***There are many awakenings within the awakening.***

Galactic channeling began a year after my Light Language experience (more about this in the Intro and upcoming *Volume 2, Scribe for the Sky*). I'm honored to have been chosen to channel ASTRID, who are 15th-dimensional blue diamond light beings. Our advanced galactic neighbors are here for our ascension, to raise our awareness to higher consciousness.

***They are here to bring us home.***

Channeled writing of encoded poetry began about a year after my introduction to light language and shortly after channeling ASTRID. The first channeled message was from my Higher Self. It flowed through me so quickly, faster than my human brain could process or write. I knew this was different, as if someone were printing the words directly into my mind.

***I am only the scribe.***

> *These words, these rhymes, may seem simple*
> *They are not scholarly*
> *Nor were they meant to be*
> *Encoded prose, encoded poems*
> *For those who are woken*
> *Those who are awake and ready to change the day*
> *Ready to create new beginnings and a new world*
> *A healed one*
> *Open and ready to receive what humanity needs*
> *And put suffering behind us*

If Light Language or channeling is new to you, I invite you to my YouTube channel (link in the back of the book) to experience it first hand. They've absolutely changed my life and they've changed the lives of the people I've shared them with.

***This is my passion and purpose.***

I welcome you to my humble home within these words. My dear soul family, I can't wait to reunite with you and re-create the beauty of a world forgotten.

## A DESTINY STORY

*How I started writing*

Many years ago, soon after my initial awakening in 2016, I drove
to Salem, Massachusetts for a circle gathering where individuals
tap into their intuition, share insights, and support one another
in developing their abilities. I wanted to practice my growing
intuition and was drawn to this group, even though it was an
hour from where I lived.

The group teacher felt familiar, yet I had never met her before.
She started us off with a simple meditation. Then we did a warm-
up exercise, but my nerves kicked in when the teacher asked the
class to break out into groups of two. We were told to "intuit"
each other and my "I'm not good enough" life theme crept up,
and fear set in. I thought, "What will happen if I get it wrong?"

Most people knew each other but I was the odd one out (yup,
the "picked last" school trauma is now on top of fear and shame
brewing in my internal emotional storm). The teacher had me
join her and another student. I was an anxious mess and had
much learning and growth to do in the years ahead.

I struggled my way through the reading, as it was my first time

doing anything like this. The teacher encouraged me, knowing
I was nervous, but I felt like I was failing another test. Looking
back, I see it was another opportunity to push myself out of my
comfort zone.

After I finished, it was time for the other student in my group to
read my energy. I will never forget what the older, wise women
said to me as she felt into my energy:

*"You're going to do something with your voice. Maybe singing,
but I also see you writing—you're a writer."*

At the time, I did not imagine I would ever use my voice,
especially since my inner voice was continually shutting myself
down. I was a designer, I used my vision to create beauty and art,
not my voice or a pen.

I remember driving home perplexed. That was the winter of
2017. Fast-forward nine years and here I am, writing a book while
also singing my soul song with Light Language.

I wish there was a way I could reach out to her and say,
"Hey, you were spot on! I'm blown away!"

*So what does this all mean?*

To me, it says that even nine years ago, someone could access my
keys, my blueprint, or my destiny—which informs me that this
was destined to happen all along. Even though I have studied
with the Modern Mystery School, found Feng Shui and many
other modalities, I still found my way to what I was supposed to
create, in perfect divine timing.

*Knowing this brings tears to my eyes,
dripping Truth down my cheeks.*

As I spoke in the preface, it wasn't until I moved to my new home that Light Language and channeling came through. After a spiritual crisis and deep lessons on boundaries, trust emerged. As with all challenges, I came out stronger than before. It opened a door to explore new levels of spirituality and healing techniques.

The day ASTRID (see Preface) came into my life is one I will always be grateful for. As I continue to practice channeling them, they always show up. It was right around the same time I felt compelled to write, as if I didn't have a choice. The words were flowing through my being and I knew I needed to capture it. However, the channeled writing in this book has not felt like the voice of ASTRID. It feels deeper and older, almost prophetic. The feeling of Thoth was definitely present, yet I have felt there were others involved. To this day, I still don't understand fully where the writing comes from. I asked who it was and I was told I didn't need to know.

What I do know is Thoth was very much a part of these transmissions and writings. For those unfamiliar with Thoth, he is known as an ancient Egyptian god of wisdom, writing, and knowledge. He is often depicted with the head of an ibis, a long-legged bird with a curved bill to represent the crescent moon. The ibis bird was considered sacred in ancient Egyptian times. The ibis symbolizes the human soul and is connected with the afterlife, with the ability to transit between the worlds of the dead and the living.

Sometimes when I channel Thoth, he refers to himself as Three, representing the sacred triangle, a sacred number, and the three doorways:
**the underworld, middle earth, and the higher realms.**

I feel a very deep connection with both Thoth and Horus, a falcon symbolizing the sky from Egyptian mythology, as if I had studied with them in another life. Perhaps this previous life as a scribe, a writer of ancient Egyptian mystery school teachings, and a preserver of knowledge, is still very much alive in me and present in this lifetime.

I also have memories of past lives as a bird avatar on another planet. As a child (and recently as an adult) I would often dream of flying. I remember one flying dream that felt beyond real when I was six or seven years old. I dreamt I floated down the basement stairs in my childhood home. The next morning, I remembered when I woke, my mom was in the basement doing laundry. I stood at the top of the stairs and told her to watch as I jumped because I could fly. Luckily, she convinced me not to. I was very angry and said, "But I did it last night!" The dream was so real I thought it wasn't a dream at all.

Even ASTRID is avian of origin. It is my understanding that they are from the constellation named the Bird of Paradise. For me, it makes sense to have this connection with all my feathered friends, both ASTRID, Thoth, and Horus. I am also connected with beautiful Isis. I took my new name, Ladybird, at her temple in 2020. Ladybird is the Great Britain term for ladybug. The ladybug has been my spirit animal and is also associated with mother Mary and good luck.

**I feel so blessed and lucky.**

## HOW TO USE THIS BOOK

I have organized my work by the date I received each download. Some arrived with their own titles, and I have honored those alongside the date.

You can read it in order and let it unfold naturally, or use it for divination by turning to a page that calls to you. I like to set an intention or ask a question, then flip through the pages until I land on one, much like shuffling oracle cards. If you love numerology, the dates and page numbers can add another layer of meaning.

You may notice throughout the poems, the capitalization of the words You or Me. This indicates the wholeness of your spirit. I go into more detail about this in my email newsletters (*find links in the back of the book*).

This book is not a literary masterpiece and it should not be read for that purpose. ***This book is more than just a book...***

*This is a sacred text.*
*It is to OPEN YOU.*

To be a transformative script—for awareness and awakening— to move through the deep emotions and let them flow.

*It is for generations to come,*
*for the Elders of the New Earth.*

It is written for the new race, the evolved human, and the new earth. There are codes within the writings to download your soul with the wisdom for your path ahead.

It's time for us to get out of our heads and into our hearts. You may have heard this from many spiritual communities already— the reason is it is the necessary next step.

**There is a reason if you were drawn to this book,
the words within are calling you.**

*They may indeed be "you" or a feeling of you
As we are all one within the Golden Sun
This is written by the collective, for the collective
You may find yourself within these words
May they fill up your soul with light
May they spark that which has been forgotten
May they remind you of who you are
A bright and love-filled shining star*

**Dear love, you have come thus far**
*Be the light for the road ahead
You never die
Bright shining light in the sky
One with the sun
This day will come
When we can all return to
Being One*

With Love.

Mary Ladybird
Spiritlight

*the*
# LETTERS

Encoded Prose
Of the Rose
Will lead
You home
To the ancient
Knowledge
Held within
It's time to
SHINE
Again, my friends

## LETTERS FROM THOTH
## TO THE NEW RACE

Move forward at your own pace
You will know which way to go
Just follow the road and follow the flow

Bring your nightlight and your pillow
Much there is to explore
It's time for you to open the new door
To the space where you have not been before

There is a new light coming
A new frequency
You just need to trust and believe
Like Peter Pan and Wendy
Take to the night sky
And you will arrive in a new land
A new Destiny at hand

You are on a journey
Yes, that is true
The journey into the new you
So go explore this new space
As you become
The new race

*Much love is to be had*
*Much love is to be explored*
*Much love through this open door*

Being in your heart, my dear ones
And journey within
Into your i-magi-nation

That is where you'll find us, you see
You really don't have to go that far on your journey
Just explore within
Go find your open door
And seek what you want to explore

With love as your guide
You will know when you have arrived
Go in peace and we will greet you
On the other side

## 3-11-2023
## THE FIRST CHANNEL

I have already experienced death
A thousand times in this life
Pieces of me fled, there is nothing left
I refuse to go on as I am, half-empty
I miss Me

This time, this opportunity
Is for the Me that was lost
That is to be found
To come back together
For the Me that wears a crown

No more losing myself, no more giving it away
I am collecting it all, right now
Today
I don't care what others think
I am enough, I won't sink
The weight in my heart is gone
I am full and I am light

Caress and love are weightless
That is all I am in my fullness
Just love—plain and simple

Simply complex—nothing & everything
I am the wind
I am no place and no thing
But I can take down mountains
Mountains of hurt, pain, and suffering
I blow those away
I settle in the field

Where my fairy friends stay
*They know me*
*They love me for who I am*

The breeze does not know disease
It blows and the trees let go
The breeze is timeless, ebbs & flows
Timeless and formless, nothing it holds
No grudges, no anger
It is free to just be—and yet it gives life to me

It gives over and over, without an agenda
*What does it ask in return?*
Nothing—just live
It's free to breathe
The essence of life is in the breath

*It's time to breathe*
*It's time to be me*
*It's time to be free*

## 3-18-2023

Are you ready to see
All that you have done throughout eternities?

You need to release to see again
The light is within you always, my friend
No matter the dark covers
Pulled over your eyes
There will be no disguise

Still point—the access to time
Time lived, time lost, time hidden in the moss
You will know it all, soon
Soon it will bloom in your mind's eye
Soon it will be uncovered
Unearthed—not pretty, but perfect

You know your job, the seeker
The seer of the unseen
Only you can unlock the doors to your dreams
To release all the unhappy you store

Courage and bravery, yes, that is required
But you will discover that
Courage lies within the darkness too
***How do you think you obtain it?***
They come in pairs ~ intertwined
Like braided hair

*The trips you have been on, the trips you will go*
*All the keys to the wisdom you secretly hold*

Carry your sword of light and all will remain bright
Go into the memories, you are a warrior of light
We need you to shine bright
You are blessed with protection
**Small but mighty**
You are surrounded by a trillion bees
Use them to pierce the dark abyss

This is the "second coming"
No time for TV, no distractions you see
It is programming you "not to be"
All that you came "to be"

Your truth, that is the focus
To move you through the challenges
Fight for your heart, fight for the divine
There is no more "time"

*Lemuria speaks through your portal*
*You see now how your heart is one with it*

You know where to go
Just take it slow and we will guide you through
The portal to the new
You

**You know what to do**
**Just be in your truth**

## 3-19-2023

Stand tall
You will not fall
Stand tall, my little one
You have just begun to grow

Stand tall
And be in your fullness
Your light is shinning
Your light is growing

Stand tall, little one
For there is much still to be done
We hold you in our hearts
As you hold us in yours

*Stand tall, little one*
*You are not little anymore*
*This is the beginning*
*This is your new door*

This is the door you have chosen
Walk through my love
***See it, believe it***
***Know it***

Be in your greatness
Step further through that door
Step fully into the light that you hold
It is gorgeous, you see
You are gorgeous, can't you see?

Stand tall
Be what you are, be it all
For your sight is
Through the crystal light
This is where you are always

*Held in this light*
*Held in this frequency*
*Held in love vibration*

Stand tall, my little one
Because you are both little and tall
You are the key to it all
Choose wisely

In time, you will learn to feel & grow
And choose with more wisdom
Being a wave, moving with flow
This is the energy you now hold

*We send our love to you, dear ones*
*My little ones and my tall ones*

We are here now to support you on this path
You have stepped into another dimension, a timeline
That is for the highest good
For the good of your soul, for your expression
Of the You that is ALL
***You my friends***...are it ALL
You hold the key—remember, you are the key to peace
Be in the vibration of peace
And humanity will be in the vibration of peace

Stand tall, my little keys
Come together
You are the swan now, you hold the beauty
You hold the dimension of above & below
Be there now
In this still point, in the quiet
In the solitude

*We hold this vibration for you*
*May you step into it*
***Step into it***

We are holding your hands
The clouds disperse, sunlight is all around you
Be still in the sunlight
As you are a beam of light

Now you shine and see
You are the tall one
You seek

**3-27-2023**

New adventures begin—a rebirth
Cutting cords and chains with the deviled one
Archangel Michael, bring your sword
And set me free for the rest of eternity

Dark Knight of the soul has passed
Another spiritual awakening, at last
More strings cut, more karma cleared
Today is the start of my new year

*I got to meet Thoth tonight at a dinner party*
*He stood over me and said*
*"Take my pen to bed and write your dreams*
*There is much more to be seen"*

## 3-28-2023

Two heads of the same stone
Who will find their glory?
One must live and one must die
I must set one free, they both cannot be
Part of the new Me
*"Why?"* I ask
Simply, it is time
It is an illusion to see things separately
If one dies, they are reborn in another timeline
Loss is only part of your reality
But not real

Anger, hatred, and pride must not reside where you are going
The role they played helped you, but no longer
Love needs to pave the way
Aim for no judgment
Just be in the bliss of what could be
This is not the end of "You"
Just the end of "me"
There is much work ahead

The snake with wings, the bird of two
That is the new You, healing you must do
May my eyes only see with Love
From high above

*On golden lips you kiss*
*It will feel like bliss*
*You will know soon dove tail*
*What true love is*

Be free to be You
Be free to collect all of You
And express the divine goddess
As the kundalini rises
Blooming the heart of the new You
Being in union with both sides
For now, enjoy the ride

## 3-29-2023
## SPEAKING WITH HIGHER SELF

ME:

*I am ready to die*
*To release the pain inside*
*Are you ready to let me go?*

HIGHER SELF:

I am You and You are Me
Together we make three
Three lives co-inside
Release these and be free

No more trauma, no more pain
Nothing left to gain
But release and let go
In time you will see
How to release
How it sets you free
How it makes you stronger
How you can stay here longer

*There is much work left to do*
*You need to be fully You*

Know I am okay
Yes, it's okay to put "me" down
Today
I'll be free at last, done with the past
History erased, making space
For the new race

*(an old lifetime haunting)*
ME:
I let go of the monster
The two headed beast
That has kept me off my feet

No more I say
Today is the
Last day you steal my name!
I am not insane!
Today
Nothing stands in my way

I let go of the past
No longer the chains
Around me
No longer they bind me

I know my strength
I know my spirit, you can't erase her
***I know my name***

## 4-7-2023

The Greys are now white
The energy has taken flight
You will know soon
What next there is to do
Some will come at noon
Till then, rest dear

*Heal and know you are clear*
*Of devils that once were*
*Now become angels up above*

Transformed, you have become
You have come to the
Sacred ground, the sacred
Ceremony Wheel
The spiral
This will take you far
Around the globe
You are free now to go
Travel with humanity
Travel with the breeze
You gypsy soul
There is more for you to know
About your ancestry
No fear
Just love at your feet

The earthly beings you will meet
The new under your feet
Will guide you where your light
Is needed, do not feel depleted

Know your strength, your courage
It's highly ranked

You got this little bird
Now fly to your tree and be heard
Sing your heart song for all to hear
This is the beginning of your new year

***Who are my new guides?***
Raphael is by your side
Gabriel has always been with you
Your new guide, you do not know
But in time they will speak to you
Yes, they speak light language too
Nothing more to do now
Nothing more to know
Curious cat

It's time to go
And show the world
Your diamond light
Your diamond heart
Shines bright tonight
Let it glow, let it flow
Let it grow

## 4-11-2023

Be in your power in this hour
You know what to do
The energy is thriving
There is no disguising
You are made to move mountains

You are at a new gate
Believe in yourself, fully
You are not too late
Just on time I would say

*Be here now and feel what the future holds*
*Don't believe what you've been told*

You are special, one of a kind
One with the rhyme
It is always your time to shine
Shine brightly, my dear
It is your year
To do great things
In little packages
Of your dreams

Cultivate slowly
Allow slow to take its place
Speed is part of the disease
You have forgotten how to breathe
***Freely, deeply, slowly***
No time or space can replace
The opportunity to be still
On the inside of you
Wear your crown and a ring

That marries you to your own king
Connection with infinity
Here you are free to escape
That trap in your mind

*Open the doors to explore*
*Another reality*

Go explore this new jungle
And discover another piece of you
The jewels of You
Add them to your crown
That surrounds your heart
When your crown is full
Of all the jewels that you are
Begin again, renewed
Carrying the healed
Aspects of You

*Allowing to live in your truth:*
*That you are nothing*
*But source*

## 4-23-2023

You are to write the new
The new testament
To what shall be
You are the queen, honeybee

*I want to live in a time when the mother knows her name*
*I want to live in a time when she knows her divinity*

The divine right to mother a child how she likes
Free and wild
Without the systems, without the dominance

What you have done to our children is wrong
There will be consequences
But I am not here to judge or pass judgment
Only to set the children free
Allowing divine mothers to hold them close
To feed them honey and toast
To heal the branches of our tree
Our past and future
Ancestry

## 4-24-2023

Mother Mary is queen bee
I love the bees
They will show you where to go
There will be a new road
The time has come for it to be undone
And re-sowed
The sky forever blue, this sky, which is you
You'll have to live in disguise
There will be secrets you have to hide
Allow love to lead the way and you will be saved
Your journey starts today

*I only light the fire*
*But you have to take the flame*
*Go after what you desire*
*There is no one left to blame*

These are your final hours
There are new ways
The time is now to change the way
Don't rely on the good old days

Morning, noon, and night
Are all opportunities for light
Join the revolution
For the divine mother is born
***Again***

*A white rose, an incarnation*
*That holds the flame and water*
*She will be our mother's father*
*An avatar*

Each toe grounds to the kingdom below
***She will know her name***
And you will know the same
Love that grows cannot be bestowed
It can be gardened into a rose
For the love of all men
She will bring peace, she will bring the end
And the beginning
***Do you know her name, as the one that holds the flame?***
Whom is the one who holds the waves
The one that balances peace
Not jealousy, not power
She will see you in your final hour
***And she will speak your name***
Then you will know
It was all just a game

The dark one of the night may try to talk to you
You will wear protection of a rose and a shield made of gold
A warrior princess of a time gone past
Wonder woman is here at last
Durga, the one who rides a tiger
She will carry you and watch over you

Innocence is a flower, a luxury of the past

*Now is the time to shield*
*Now is the time to yield*
*Now is the time to love*
*Now is the time to heal*

No longer do you need to kneel
All you need to do is love

Remember that first and above all
You will not fall

*Stand tall, stand tall*
*My little honey bee*
And all will be well
Drink from the well of the honey blossom
Raise your vibration
And blossom

## 4-27-2023

Baby bird, so far from its nest
With no place to rest

Scary world out there, all alone
So far from what was home

Knowing nothing, feeling extinct
From the world it used to know
That has sinked

*Baby bird, flap your wings*
*You know, it's only a dream*

So far from reality
This is why you feel like fleeing
Wanting an escape
Making it hard to
***Breathe***

***Baby bird***
Look where you reside
Two feet on the ground
But you must learn to fly

You are whole on the inside
This you must know
You have not lost your place
In this new race

Be free, baby bee
Stretch your wings
Feel the wind underneath

There is strength in them
To carry you through a new door
This opportunity awaits, do not delay
Take flight, today

**///**

Go be a little fish, dive into your bliss
Finding a new way to play
This is your day
Go deep into the sea
There, on the floor, awaits your destiny
Yes, you have been there before
A different time, a different space
Get to know your original race
Paint your face with gold
Embrace what you have been told
Get to know the old
You
Your ancient self
A fish in the clay

*Mold it to what you are today*
*Mold a new you, a new face*
*You are the golden race*

The gold lies deep within
Peace is right around the corner
***Know Thyself***
It lies within the corridor
Between the magic and the lore
One foot in, and one foot out
One step to take
To that magic space
The beauty of the present day

## 5-8-2023

Dipping volcanic ash into copper, then gold, is in the past
Time to discover and uncover the truth at last
Dissolve away the old
Be here now, in this new energy, behold!
A King, a Queen, yes, they will all sing
When they see with the new eyes
All of the old lies
Baptized in the new truth
Do not lead a false prophecy
We are here to help you lead them
To the coming Golden Age

*///*

I see your glow
In the shadow night
There is something there
I know it's not right
A portal, perhaps
No, it has collapsed
A dragon, mighty and brave
Perhaps, but not today
My cat goes and visits you
Every night
He knows something is not "all right"
Or does he see Light
And I only see darkness
The pedals fall
Before their time
Something out of sync
Something doesn't rhyme
*I saw your glow*

Like rain from a rainbow
You give life even in the dead of night
That which is special and unseen
*What is behind your mystery?*
In order to know, I must die
To see that which is reflected in my cats eyes


*III*


Your dreams spell
What is lurking
No tea to spill
Only the deceased can freely see
The demon that exists within me

I ask:
*Is God a demon or a priest? Perhaps both?*
*Must they meet to remove the evil bound to me?*
*What must I do to remove*
*That which is part of the whole?*
*I feel empty and old*

THEM:
The truth be told
We all are beauty and the beast
Does this scare you? Perhaps it should
But that is just a fever from another time
It is just an old rhyme

ME:
*What I want to know*
*Is how the future will be told*
*Which version of truth will be recorded*
*And read by our youth?*

THEM:
This is the time to write what is mine
My story, my perspective of what is truth
Do you have time in a pocket in space
To share about the new race?
This is the time, it is the plan
Mary is part of the story
The writer and creator
The mother too, for all of you
Soon you will see what is meant to be
Have trust and faith in me
I will lead you to a new home indeed
A world where kindness is valued
More than paper, no more need to rape her
Mother Gaia
Do not throw in the towel
We love you, but don't show it
I would be fed up, this is true
But no, your children love you

*Through all your layers of time and space*
*Please help show us the new way*

Gaia says, "Be kind to each other,
Every day, in every way
Children you already know the way
It will happen, keep the faith
Be the cure to your own disease
You are free
Now just truly believe."

You are the bee and the beekeeper
Honey in the hive
May you keep her

Safe until it's time
To allow her to fly to the next bee keeper
Then it will be time to give the keys
Up to the sky, heaven's gates awaits your arrival
Do not wait, fly through the golden door
There is so much in store

No need to rush, as you are on time
So much to re-remember
So much to reiterate
You have time to pass through the second gate
Just know you are never too late
To grow old and wise
Youth they say
We are born with wrinkles of all our timelines
This life is just one big wave
Which all crashes one day
Into one million micro waves

*Across the sands of time*
*Across this span of space*
*We will all dissolve into one race*

With no face, just time
To float throughout space
We are all particles of time
Weaving in and out of each other
To create the stories and statues
To remind us what we came to do
***To just exist***
That is at the top of each of our wish list
In whatever form
In whatever way
Good, bad, happy, sad

Suffering or jubilation
The ability to feel is the freedom we seek

*And yet we drown ourselves*
*To sleep in this waking dream*

May we all be seen
To be clear of mistakes
Of the previous human race
You must know, dust is not your home
You are free to roam
You have had many bones, many homes
But this one needs you to awaken
***Have this woken dream***
***Stand tall and be seen***
Don't allow the fall to take you downstream
Believe in your dream
Behind the waterfall, we wait
To feed you a feast
For overcoming your inner beast
There is so much to do
Get to work on the new you
Step up and take your seat
Enjoy the food that feeds the new you
Knowing your love is what feeds us all

***Stand tall***
***Have no fear***
The pieces will fall exactly how they are meant to, my dear
Don't lament over this event
Be bright in your truth
The goddess sees you
Use this to paint a new future, a new life
Rewrite the past to allow the present to be heard
Hear her speak your words to life

**5-26-2023**

Let it flow, let it bloom
See yourself in a new room
Hour by hour, you'll learn of your power
The power of draining your pain
Becoming whole again
Allow in your true vibration
Before all these incarnations
Remove the idea of all these nations
We are one earth, we all deserve
Freedom to roam, no house, no home
Your true nature is to heal this earth
Travel to all your places of birth
These people You have been
Are all part of
The You
Integrate all that you've been
Become friends with all of your selves
They are true and part of the You
Yes, the shadow lifetimes too
They are the circle of truth
That completes the full You
Know this is the
*TRUTH*

*Stop running away from time and space*
*They are all part of the You*
*Right here, right now*
*In the Today*

Access and integrate Them with care
Know them and release once they have been seen
You free these parts of You to be healed

Send them unconditional love
For the lessons, the pain
As it is all rewarded on another plane
The multidimensional "You" knows the
***TRUTH***

Come to your heart space
It is time to become part of time & space
To be of a new race
Going beyond, the beyond
Enlightenment is the new race
This must take place
Do your part—create
With the spark in your heart
Transform into this new energy
You are already there, my sweet dear ones
Just meet us halfway and we can bring you
All the way to safe shores
Just walk through the doors
To this beauty in-between
This time and space
We've got you

*Let's embrace with all the love*
*From below and above*
*Fear—no longer, that time is up*
*Be free to be in*
*Love's eternity*

## 6-2-2023

You are the star that will lead the way
For the return of the holy child
An oracle of the light
That shines brightly in the night
The light in the void
Shines the way for the new day
***Do not delay!***
The journey starts right away

*Divinity in a day, divinity in an hour*
*Divinity is the power*
*Be here, now wholly, fully*
*The divine mother is calling you*

She will show you what you need to do
Allow the Seraphim to shine bright
Tonight is your night

Be the tree upside down, blossoming underneath
Blossoming through your toes, through your feet
Into the New Earth, in the ancient ways
New knowledge, new healing happening today

Be aware, small one, what is under your feet
They are waiting to greet you
The tall trees, the tall ones
Will cure our disease

## 6-14-2023

Divine rising of the tale of two heads
That awaken the dead
Bring peace to the Earth
A new land, we will birth
Removing shadow from this place
Do not take haste
Perhaps two tails and one head
Would come instead
The truth will set you free
**Be in your divinity**

*As sure as the eagle flies*
*The Serafin is by my side*

*Do you know your true identity?*

You hold your greatest power
In your darkest hour
Integrate the monster
Integrate the love
And come out above her
There is a divine mother
Eight - O - Eight
You open that gate
As a reset to a new life
To abundance and all that is right

**"Sleep well tonight**
**There are big plans ahead**
**Beauty within the beast "**
That is what she said

Now, lay your head down, sweet one
And rest

The initials in Mona Lisa
Lady in disguise — LD
*Lady Diva*
*Lady Divine*
*Lady Divinity*
You will see her in time
And the clock strikes 11 (*9*)
She will be sent to heaven
The magic number 27
You'll understand when you go
Mystery you seek is within you
The mystery you seek is the beast
*— Unlocked*

*AUTHORS NOTE*
*As with most of these poems, this speaks in layered symbolism rather than direct meaning. Numbers and phrases may point to states of awareness rather than fixed meaning.*

*"11 (9)" and "27" mark moments of transition — where endings, beginnings, and integration meet. The "Lady Divine" is not separate, but something revealed over time, often hidden in plain sight.*

*What appears as mystery, shadow, or even the "beast" is not outside of you, but part of what is being integrated. Meaning unfolds gradually, as recognition arises from within.*

*This is not something to solve, but to recognize. Allow these codes to dance off your tongue in joyful pleasure as you are not only reading — you are remembering.*

## 6-15-2023

Numbers and sequence
So easy it seems
With just a glance
A gleam of the unseen
A moment in time
In this rhyme
Is sound on paper

*Music in the elevator*
*Singing the collective*
*Soul of Silence*

"Know your worth"
Is a sentence you hear
*But what do you think you deserve?*
*What number is your thoughts?*
As they get lost
Downstream
Forgetting your dreams

*Sequence your life*
*The numbers will follow*
*Truth be told*
*By the hoot of an owl*
*The sequence of time*
*Lies in this rhyme*

Know your numbers
And be seen
So you can live
Your best dream
It is not the wave

That takes you away
But the current that lies
In the dark sea underneath

Do not delay
Know your work today
And float along the ocean floor
As you create in the dark
Returning to the sea
Where you were born
Where you are formed
Into your greatest
Potential

## 6-25-2023

Know where you are going
Time leads the way
To the new day

*Time by your side always*
*No need to delay your heart*

She is the truest part of you
That is not confused

There is only now, this moment, always
***And yet,***
Change is ***always*** happening

Do not delay
As time is neither here or there
It's ***always*** time
To be your best self

## 7-7-2023

*There's a gold mine under my feet*
*Hidden under the Roman columns that you seek*
*But it is not gold you are looking for*
*It is Christ Divinity*

You did not need to go far
You can stay where you are

Heaven for us all, small or tall
We all come together
We are one song, one harmony
***Of Love, peace, trust***
***This is a must***

Light workers of the New World
Must remove the snakes from the lake
Where the sun turtles come to bake
The trolls must go under the bridge
Back to where they live
Yet they need to bring *love* along the way
Or they too, shall decay

*Bring the sun with you, my friends*
*And let it light the cave*
*There's nothing left to slay*
*Your light shines bright and leads the way*

The time is now, do not delay
Bring on the new day

The three lines in the triangle
Each one representing Unity of the whole
Coming together to form beauty
The triangle is a road trip, coming to get her
DaVinci knows this
And why it's so mysterious

## 7-9-2023

The door is open
Don't be afraid of death
But of an unlived life
Death to engage life
Remembering bones, our stones
Memories held in
Crystals, the bones
Of the Earth
A  open door to sacred spaces
*Listening*

Everything is alive

*What does sacred time look like?*
*What is the message of a crow?*
*"Where is the elder of this land?"*
*I must know*

Rub hands with soil
By the river
Then rinse in water and say your name
And give an offering

Walk in peace among the chaos
Older, closer to remembering
Don't fret over the Earth
*Love it*
It's leading you back
*Inside*
To exist
As a collective

## 7-11-2023

It's time to live
In the space between
Dreams *and* earth *and* heaven

*You are one with all that is*
*This is where you shall live*
*In the in-between dreams*
*Real and unseen*

Magic, pure and simple
Know yourself as I know you
This dream you will pursue

***Spirit loves you***
***Know this well***

Time will tell as you pass the tests
That are ahead, and behind you
Awaken and asleep
This is the world you keep
And your waking consciousness

Live true, and life will find you
Between the swan's wings
Is the key to everything
Masculine beauty
Keeper of the heart song
She will find her partner before long

*Lay the golden egg*
*Of a new age ahead*

**From the devils that had you bound**

You have your wings now
Together fly
No matter the weather
Be at each other's side
Hold each other's hand

**Sacred love**
With blessings from above

## 7-15-2023

This prose is healing the old
Creating a new song to be sung
Right from wrong
The mask is undone

*Sing free, my little songbird*
*Singing your new song*
*Sing proudly, as you can't go wrong*
*Sing for all things*
*Sing for beauty*
*Sing for peace and love divine*
*Sing for a new time*

A rose floating in the sea
No longer
It is grounded deep
And it flowers
Opens its petals
Exposing the pollen
Stand still in this Unity
With man and femininity
Standing still
**Open**
Allowing it to find you

This is divinity
Divine love
Unite the masculinity
Take back all the love that has been lost
In a desert of frost
Melt away
As the touch of sun

*Opens the flower*
You are now in your power
Divine union

When I am ready
I shine my divine light on the heavy
I will go to the dark water
I will shine my light
It will be seen from shore to shore
Dark shadows, see the light
Integrate
Be free
Be not afraid
As the light of source
Sees you
Knows you, too
Take off the shadow mask
It is a role you no longer need to play
It is judgment day
And you too, can bask in the light
That you've been afraid to look at

*Shadow, do not feel shame*
*You were just playing a game*
*Shadow, do not look away*
*Shadow, you are part of me*

That is divinity
Shadow, lighten your load
No need to carry the heavyweight
For it is the Golden Age
Where we're all in Union
Together as One

## 7-17-2023

The time is at hand
To be shown the way into the new day
Above and below
All is right here
To access without fear
To know thyself fully and completely
The new day has come to greet me

Trust, have faith, you will be shown the way
Do not fear destruction on your path
It breaks your chains
To be free at last
Free to live your best life without disease
Freedom to really do what you please
This is part of the healing cure
**Open that door**

You must rid yourself of the rage
Unfairness causes pain
Free yourself of these chains
And you will see **change**
No longer living a life
Based on society's games
Of gathering titles and promotions

*What is your devotion?*
*What if the unseen work*
*Is really becoming advanced humans?*

The work is to hold more love and joy
To learn forgiveness and boundaries

*What if the reward was really kindness?*
To heal past life karma
To learn compassion

*What if this was the true measure of success?*
Re-organize the old programming
To this new way

**7-22-2023**
## PROPHECY OF THE ROSE

The key is **You**
Move through the gate
Through the rose
Water tunnel
Here you go
Pass the sword
Pass the moon
Through time and space
To build the new race

*You are the portal*
*You are the key*
*To bring back to you*
*What you seek*

The path ahead
May be hard
Stay in your heart
Oceans away
You are okay

Use *love* as your sword
There is strength in yours
Be brave and allow
Spirit to lead you
To the highest form of **You**

## 7-27-2023

The time has just begun
Bird on the fence
You have chosen your defense
Time to fly away
Be free in this new way
No more sitting, waiting
Your wings lead you

Above and below
There are three, but there are five
In the fifth dimension they fly
Don't throw in the towel
The darkness will cleanse you
And the divine light will rebirth you
Oh, come out of the bath waters
Grab a new towel
Come into Bethel Israel

*Eyes that are blue*
*Eyes that are new*
*Guide the way*
*In my new day*

Chariot has arrived
The birth of a new child
From the divine mother womb
You will know her soon

## 7-31-2023

In this living dream
Nightmares can appear
*How do you escape?*
Slow down, take your place
It is part of the human race
"X" marks the spot

*Is Jesus here?*
He's everywhere, my dear
He can clear the nightmare
And return you to a state of bliss
You decide if that is the ride you want to be on

I release this emotional weight to the well
No longer do I need to carry it all
I lighten my load for humanity
I leave an empty vessel, open for the new
It's time to plant my seeds
It's time to grow
In new soil

Bring home the vibration from the well
The emptiness will tell
Of a new story, a new road
*Be here now, be in your glory*
A new journey has begun
Without the snakes, without the tangles

*Be the joker and be set free*
*The fool, if you must be*
*But start ahead on your journey*
*With the magicians wand*

That is the signpost you should follow
Remember, you are not really hollow
The emptiness in life that you see
*Is really filled with the light*
*With the potential to be*
*Your new tomorrow*

They will come and you will follow
You can be both a leader for tomorrow
And a student, all at the same time
You have stepped into a new game
The path of ascension is before you
You've opened the door
You've stepped through

*Now go on your adventure*
*Go and be free*
*To explore your new "me"*

Master your emotions, and you will see
The brightness shining on the river
The joy and the glee
Remember this moment always
As it will go either way
When you are having troubled days
Really see the love that you have

You have passed all your tests
Now go and rest
In the bliss of what is ahead

## 8-2-2023

Love is love
From above and below
You will know where to go

This is not a test
You have done your best
It is not time to go
Just time to slow
Find your heart
That is where to start

If you are lost along the way
Start a new song today
A sweet tune
To turn things around

Beautiful bee
Fly free

## 8-6-2023

A new vision for a world not yet come
Hold it close to you and it will be
*"How" you ask?*
You will see the sun in the sky
No longer hide
The truth it holds
A new story needs to be told

*What if the Hindu deities' arms*
*Represent all the different energies*
*Becoming one?*

*If I imagine all my arms, what energies do I hold?*
*Maybe it isn't about passions, healing, or jobs*
*What if our path is to unfold*
*Using the divine life forces*
*We each hold?*

**8-8-2023**
ARIEL *(Cindy's Harmonic Egg)*

Come rest in me
Dear ones, let me be your nest
Allow to rest and reset
Raining frequency
***Relax in me***

Allow the waves of sound
To wash away your frown
***Reset***
Reset your spirit
Your crown

*Let go and let me hold you*
*Like a mother*

I will cradle you
I will sing you sweet songs
Heal now, sweet babe
Come inside so we can play
All will be okay

*Hey Love,*
*What do you have for me today?*
*What words of wisdom do you say?*
Remove confusion from your past
You are free to create your destiny at last

Remove your fear and be clear
For clarity is here
Illumination, my dear
Is just through the doorway of Love
*Of Love, of Love*

Sing your song of freedom
Sing your song of love alive
You are alive
Smile brightly and feel that joy inside
*Your Soul, your Soul, your Soul*

*Hey Love,*
Be the light that leads your way
To a new day coming
Where we all know
The beauty, the power, the wisdom
*Of Love, of Love, of Love*

*Bright as a dove in sparkling sun
Dotting the sky with sparks of peace*

Release your beasts, hiding in the dark
Just beneath the sparks
Show them your fearless heart
That cannot die

No where left to hide, all must rise
*RISE, RISE, RISE*
See to release, get to know your beast
They need to be seen
To be heard, written in the world
Release from me, it's safe to be seen
*And Rise, and Rise, and Rise*

Rise in consciousness beyond the emptiness
Of space & time
And rise with this rhyme
With Love from your soul

## 8-12-2023

My soul sound is healing
Beyond humanity
Beyond this reality
It is soft, yet strong
Ancient and wise
It's lead by my guides
And truth in my heart
That knows where to start
It lives in other worlds
Behind closed doors
That are opened to be shared

*Love is a sound*
*You make in your heart space*
*This soul is beyond*
*Any race*

Know its wisdom will set you free
Feel it in your eternity
It needs to be shared
Open your eyes and your ears
To feel the sound in your core
Be there, inside the corridor
To the sacred space
Where creation lives
In that empty space
Waiting to see what you
Are going to say

*SING YOUR TRUTH*
Truth—this soul
Yearns for eternity

Sacred space
Know your truth

***Sing it now***
She knows you
Feel her and be
Your wholeness
Set free

## 8-17-2023

Be free, little bee
You know where you will go
It may feel slow
But you will know
That all will be okay

This day you can play
And be in the breeze
*Of ease*
*Breathe free*
*Honeybee*
*You are in love*
We have heard your wishes from above
*Love freely*
No need to escape the feelings
Allow them in your being
The good, the bad
Happy or sad
Allow them to flow through
You will know what is right for you

Be free, honeybee
To explore this world of possibilities
No need to fear
Change is already here
To lead you to new doors
Of peace

**8-18-2023**

Feathered wings
Bring a new dream
Allowing yourself to sing
Songbird, you are

*Breathing beauty into the world*
*Sound creation at the time of your birth*

Waves of creation
Water in air
Breath, new and breath, extinct
Even sound has death
Silence takes over
**Rest**
**Pause**
**Recharge**
Come back to your
**Self**
**Alive**
Ready to inhale
And start again

My friend
Remember your sound ripples
***What is your song made of***
***—butterfly wings?***
***Is it the sound of your dreams?***

Flutter now with the
Sound of hope
It is the sound you make
Vibrating the new heaven

Being one with both
Creating the world
As we speak
Know this truth
Allow it to resonate
Within you

*Sing this song*
*In your dreams*
*Creating a new world*
*In the unseen*

A new reality
Co-create
Your sound is alive
Has no limits
Breathe new life
Your chance is now

Allow your heart to sing
There is beauty in your song
You can't get it wrong

Be free, feathered friends
With joy or sorrow
With courage or shame
Express what you need
Spirit will carry it
To the realm of eternity
To resolve or release
The beast you do not need
Its time has come to also be released
**No more heaviness**
**No more shame**
**No more guilt**

All can be erased
Yes, this will be the new race
Ones that come without the heavy
Weight of doubt
The fear virus removed and cleared

**You did it, my dear!**
In this space and time, in this now reality
Imagine how it will be
Take me home
To this place
I want to roam

Allowing love to guide my way
To this new day
**Here**
**Now**
It is all okay
We love you, dear ones
Know this wisdom

*What ever challenges you face*
*We are here loving you anyway*
*You are doing all there is to do*
*Float freely and we will guide you*

This Truth is not the end
But just the tip of the iceberg, my friend
So much depth for us to explore
Open this door
You know you can
We will hold your hand
Laying the foundation for others to come
Your ancestors of the future

Lives here in this world you create
By opening the door
To deeper wisdom
The universe you create
Is waiting for you
To explore

Now go create that new life
It awaits your arrival

## 9-1-2023

Muddy waters, running clean
Change this nightmare into a dream
Of new beginnings
What's ahead has never been seen
For humanity

Look under your feet
It is all green
A New Earth is being birthed
But first it must run through the cave
Shown the shadows of the old
So then you can emerge
The mound will see it first
The new day, the new birth
Mount Zion and Jerusalem
*Must change*

A fire burning great from the torch of new light
Great ones will emerge
With the help of masters
*They will come*
Like the Robin in the spring time
Coming out of hiding
Bringing a new song to sing
To awaken an old dream
That's a time that's past
We thought it was going to be here and last

*"How may we help," you ask?*
Look to your blue heart and heal the past
It's time to let go of those phases
Truly, be in the New Earth, now

Forge a new path to the waters edge

*A new shore awaits you*
*Grab a paddle and spirit grabs the other*
*Together, creating greatness*

It may look like a long journey ahead
But the best way forward is one stroke at a time
Focusing on your rhythm and rhyme
It will pass the time
And soon you'll be on your way
A smoother ride ahead
One experienced
Like the stillness of a turtle on a log
You too, will overcome the fog

Be still always
**Remember who you are**

**9-2-2023**

Temple
*Heal the wounds of the dead*
*Heal the past versions of me*
*Feed me the new light codes*
Help me heal this frustration and anger
Of jealousy and rage
I don't want these any longer
Remove them right now, right away
I bathe in the new waters
I bathe under the gates
Of the new energy
*Please integrate*

I release the moonstone to the Earth mound
She holds the old and the new energies that abound

*The only one I am married to is Spirit*
*The Me, the You, and I*

The diamond is inside of You
Made of blue
Playground for all three
To live and breathe
Soon you will see the forest for the trees
And all the spirits that surround you

Be in discernment, day by day
You will find your way
To perceive those around you
As diamonds or disease

The beauty and the beast story has ended
A love will drown in the abyss

No longer in my grasp, it belongs in the past
As I walk through these gates
*A new race*
*At a new pace*
*With more grace*
*More flow*
*More going slow*
A tug here or there from spirit
Unleashed from the beast
You must trust in a new vision
And allow for revision

Remember, the gems are within you
A diamond found in the trash
Will shine and gleam
And come out to the surface and be seen

This old road, you no longer have to go
Follow your vision
Love it, bloom it to fruition
Go to the mountain tonight
Go inside and see its light
Its temple, so bright
Release all fears in this place
In this temple, you'll remember my face

This palace of light
Shines so bright
Emanating your light
From sea to sea
A flame will burn for me
It is the wisdom seekers
The wisdom seers that hold the flame
You are now one in the same

## HI-CHI, VENUS SPOKE TO ME—
## A MESSAGE TO HUMANITY

*Now this my friends—*
The world is not coming to an end, just merely changing
frequency. You will know this in time and understand the
necessity for your evolution.

Be quiet so the work can be done.
Know we are here assisting you.

*Take heed—*
For there will be changes in your energy, for we are beauty and
butterflies and we want you to fly!

Love messengers are all around you. *Tap into them.*

*Stay awake!*
We see you slipping away and we are here to say
"Wake up to a new day!"

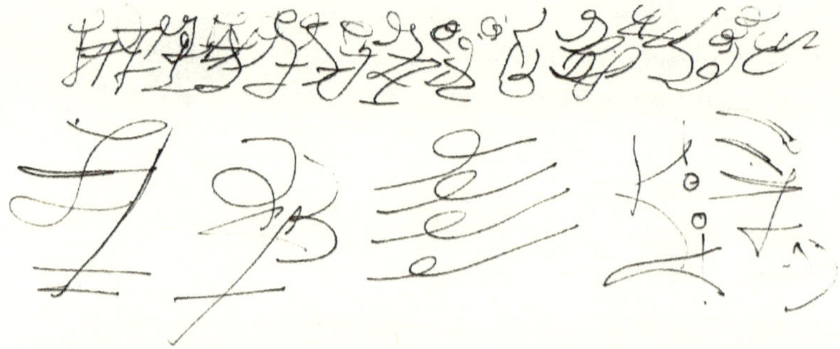

*I am the collector of souls in the wind*

## 10-2-2023

Destiny, re-hook me
Being free is fun but I still need direction

*Which destiny do I choose?*
The one that is of highest good for all
Destiny hooks and unhooks throughout your life
Depending on your timeline
Sometimes, the skyhook attaches to you
To bring you up a level
Sometimes, when you're in the woods
And off the path
The skyhook will bring you back
And lead you to the right path forward

*Are we not allowed to create*
*And build our own way?*
Yes, that is what you're doing
Through your destiny
The seasons are just metaphors for your life
They open and close doors
The seasons change and rearrange
And are used as a guiding post
For you to make the most
Of your garden and your seeds

*What will bloom? What will die?*
*What will have disease?*
These, too, are all metaphors you see
As you are all just true divinity
Nothing more, nothing less
Yes, you have passed another test
Listening to your soul's light

*Listen*
*You can hear it take flight?*

Truth be told, there is divine all around you
Listen softly, with your eyes closed halfway
You'll see the opening, the gateway
Follow through it and be free
Follow through it
It leads to your destiny

The awakened one
She was baptized today
In the rain, by the rain
It's taking days, not weeks
Soon you will meet
She is the thunder inside of you
Your hips do ache
This life, not a piece of cake

*Hurry now, do not be late*
*Alice in Wonderland*
*You have defeated the evil queen*
*Even if it was in a dream*

Rise to the surface
Rise and do your part
Rise and know your heart
Rise back to your bed
Where you lay your sleepyhead
And awake

A new one arises, a being born from the spine
It happened in an old time
In an old rhyme

You no longer need to hold this pain
There is nothing left to gain
From going through it again
I release it now to heaven
The old myth, the old stories
The old ways of seeking a "glory"
Ride free on a horse's back
Allow the wind to pull it from you

*No longer yours*
*Release the snakes*
*Release the heartache*
*I give it to the river*

Allow the two heads of the dragon
To become one
Allow this merging to be done
No longer two heads are needed, just one
I release the gator in the well
No more children to feed it
*It is a new age*
*Let us see it*

*I let it go*
*I defeated it*
It will no longer be in my Temple
It is no longer part of my home
It is no longer part of me
For all eternity

## 10-5-2023

I hold the torch in the fire
A new day is what we desire
Allowing the flame to be seen
Much light to be gleamed

May the old see the flame too
And know that the new day is upon us
The flame burns the old away
Showing the way to a new day

*The new birth, of a new child*
*She is on her way*

Burning away the old you
Allowing in the new
The queen that resides
From the old ancient ways
Coming back to birth a new day
A new race
Weaving together the old and the new
Allowing the old to slow
Births a new queen
To rule this earth

She will be born, both male and female
A bridge to the new ways
We are building that today
Wood and water come together
Building a bridge
That releases the old stories
And gives way to a new light
The new flame, she shines bright

***Steady and true, you will find each other***
***And birth a new world***

The flame of the snake is the medicine
Do not mistake
Over the Golden Gate
There is a chair
For the queen
Bring together fire and earth
Queen bee, sit here
And you will be birthed
A bridge between realities
There are no u-turns
But in the life between
That's all there is
A folding onto oneself
A folding together of the two into one

Queen, you have "one"
One life to live, one birth to give
***Live fully***

*Your home is in the woods*
*Your home is by the sea*
*Your home is everywhere you will be*

## 10-21-2023

Holding the medicine of the new ways
To heal the old days
This is your gift, you are the star, you are the seed
That humanity needs
Be on the way little one, blowing in the wind
Yes, this is the journey, take it in
The baby in the cradle is the New Earth
The baby is the Earth being born again
Mary's birth was for the Earth
*And then Jesus came*

This flower torch, you are
Burning brightly, now, like a brand new star
Lower your gaze
It will take your breath away
The flame in the water grows the rose
To bloom from stone
Allow the hardness to cease
You have tamed that beast
Walk away, head held high
Walk away, with the gaze towards the sky
As it is just a mirror for you to see yourself
*Clearer*

I love the beauty of the flame
Helping you remember your name
*Goddess, Mother, Mary*
But this isn't her story
This is yours to have and to hold and to grow
Into the blooming rose of your higher self
The past is rectified, now go on your way
*Create that new day*

## 11-27-2023

FEAR:
Do you know her name?
They said that she went insane

ME:
*No, I don't know her name*
*Who is it that you are trying to blame?*

FEAR:
It is Fear, that is me
I won't rest for eternity

ME:
But what I hear is you want rest
don't you think that's best?

FEAR:
*Yes, but where will I get my energy?*

THEM:
I give you now, to the sun
The sun will hold you, the sun will feed you
The sun will allow you to rest
Until you can shine it's light again
We have needed Fear for many years
No longer do we need fear
It's time for you to transform as well

ME to FEAR:
Leave my body where you dwell
Leave now and know you will be at peace
My child, will greet you, with Grace

Leave me, leave all of me
Leave me and let me be the new Me
Leave for all eternity until you are needed again
In the form of light from the sun, shining bright
To you Fear—I say good night

I send you to the light
*Remove from my hip now*
*Remove from my cells*
*Remove from my brain waves*
And all will be well
Within the eclipse energy
When the sun and the moon become one

*This is the time you will leave me*
*And two will become one*

THEM:
A line between the new and the old
Planting a seed to be sowed
The line of divinity in the soil
To bloom, new branches
In new flowers to be
Along the edge of the sea
The merging of land and ocean
There is a devotion
A wanting, a need
To return to the Sea of eternity
Thus, you will build a new home for yourself
A new home for humanity
Building a new home with the capital being Rome
*You will see the divinity within the hour*
*You will see the divinity within the flower*
The blue flower of the eyes

The eyes of Divine
The eyes that always shine
What comes, may come
Pray this old world be undone
Unweaved, unwoven
Allowing a new story to be told
Of a child in a blue manger
A new Joseph, a new Mary
The divine family reunited
The divine feminine reborn
I am the star in the manger
In the night when she was born
I am the star and the mother
Together, we have sworn

*Secrets—secrets we must keep*
*The child must live, the child*
***—we must meet***

When the time is right
All will see
How she brings in the new humanity
Living in peace, brothers and sisters
***You will know her name***
***No, this is not a game***

*You will know her as Lady Grace*
*She is the baby that forms the new race*

ME:
As her mother
In this moment
***I erase hate***
***I erase loneliness***

*I erase hatred, harm*
*I erase all that is of not the highest light*
So I may step into this new world
So I may cross this bridge
Releasing all of me that there is
All of me that is of old energy
And I cross into a new life
I cross over tonight
*My will be done*
*A new me has come*
A star that will light the Way
Go without pride, without shame
Only the new "Free Will" resides

THEM:
*Rainbow children, my friends*
My daughters, my sisters, my brothers
Esoteric blood from another
Mix with the wine, out of time
*Mother of the rose divine*
Burn your wilted flowers away
Burn them into the blood of the divine
Burn them with the blood of the child that is mine
My blood, your blood
Together they mix
To form a new bliss

It's been on your wish list
To create a new world
A safe place, a harbor
Yes, a last-minute change of plans
We're going to the new place, the new land
Where you will be a helping hand
A creator, your soul

Your Creatrix, a plan
For the new land
Follow the light, follow the new way
Follow the lights in the sky
Who are the stars that guide
Humanity out of this roller coaster ride
Sing your song, loud and true
Sing yourself
***Brand new***

**12-1-2023**

We thank the women of the ancient past
For coming and grounding the feminine
Blooming now for our divinity

They held the secret ways
They brought forth the new days
Their time is gone, but not forgotten
As the lady slippers bloom
Under their grave

*Lady slippers, show your face*

Show the essence of your race
Show us how it's meant to be
In divine femininity
We know your energy is ancient
We know your soul is divine
Open your pedals
And show us your smile
Releasing your beauty, your power
As we watch you, as you open
Your womb, your blooming
*Eyes*

Lead us through
The portal
Of divine feminine
*Love*

## 12-8-2023

We don't change colors
That you see
Human vision is limited
In expression
Due to repression

*New knowledge is what you seek*
*The answer lies under your feet*

Be one with the sun
She will shine the way
But you must remember how to play
With energies surrounding you
As you speak
This is not a huge feat to complete
Allow the flow, see the waves in the sky
They will teach you how to fly
Towards your dreams that are still unseen

Be here now and we will carry you
Along your way
You were meant to show the way
For others to explore
Their true nature within

The deep waters call you
***You know the way***
A time that has passed, but still is
A refuge, a place of imagi-nation
Open that door in 2024
A land of discovery awaits
Remembrance will take place

*Bring your beauty in*
*Take a bath in it, allow it to sink in*
*A land of image-nation*

Lead the way to a land of play
And you will see the great shifts
In humanity
**Be strong and proud**
Negativity is not allowed
**Be strong and proud**
You have already "made it"

And yet, this is not the end
Only an evolution of the spiral, my friends
Go in peace that you seek
It is right here
At your feet

## 12-15-2023
## ELDERS OF THE NEW EARTH

The elders of the Earth are ready to birth
A new way forward from the center
The Galactic Center is also within
That is where the birthing begins
Traveling from other worlds
The elders sing their old songs
They are wise and strong
The elders remember, the power of the dark
That is within your heart
That gives birth to new light
Remember there is power in the night

There is nothing to fear
The night is just day without light
You will feel whether this is right
Now is the time to look deep within

*Where are your roots? Where are they growing?*
*What is the soil beneath your feet?*
*How can you water those roots that grow into your tree?*

There it lies, within the magic
Tend to your roots, children of this Earth
Look back to your birth
Yes, you may come from different worlds
You have them in your bones, however, you know
On some level that this is also your home
Some of you been here through the centuries
Whether you've been here once or multiple times
This is still your home
*So be here*

Yes, you are free to roam
*But be here*

There are lessons you must not fear
There are lessons you cannot escape
That is the plan, so as you channel, do not escape
As you channel what is best for the human race
*Be here now*

*Do not take its place among the stars just yet*
*There are many things that you forget*
*That need to be remembered*

*For healing, for learning*
*For wisdom*
*For growth of the soul*

*Be here now*
Child of young and old
*Be here now*
The story has been told

## 12-31-2023

The dream team believes in you
And all that you do
No more fear, let's be clear
Step into not "how" but "why should I"

*Love is behind you*
*Pushing*
*Forward motion*
*Propelling change*

The last day of 2023
Time to let go of the past
Design a new consciousness
As above, as below
As the saying goes

It will bloom at noon
Not far is the star
Love is on the way
Time to awake into a new state

Believe and you will see
The new inside of you
It awaits your arrival
It's soon
Plant the seed
And it will be
Never lost

## 1-1-2024

As the dragon's eyes glow
As a rose pedal opens
This is a passage from heaven

*Know how to close*
*Your eyes and go inside*

Be one with the flow
Be one now, the new You will know
Which way to flow
Without a watch, there is no clock
That can tell you when
Your future will begin
Follow the flow, the rhythm of your heart
That will lead the way to your new day
**A *beginning***
Of time without time or rhyme
But just the beat of your wave of energy
There will come a time, out in space
Of a new race
It may feel like an eternity away
But it will be present, within a day

Yes, you are on your way my friends
Look for the new beginning
And you will know which way you are to go

Beauty awaits in every moment
Like a mystery to be found
I am whoever you want me to be
***Can't you see, you are awesome?***
Infinite infinity

Release the bonds that keep me down
Release the chains
Allow me the freedom to play and explore
Open up all my doors
To the beauty that awaits

New worlds to explore
I am ready to travel the path not crossed
No fear, I won't get lost
I have carried my own cross
I let go that which I have lost
*I allow the past to be that*
*I allow the future to guide me*
*I allow the present to find me*
And within that realm
*I allow myself to be found*

*Beautiful people,*
Remember to ground
Your starlight into Gaia
As you forget, remember
She is a star just like you
Ready to bloom
Your light to shine
Bright into the galaxy night
Love Divine

*Little bird, take flight*
Shine that light, day or night
Sing your way into the new day
Things will start to go your way
*Beautiful love birds*
Shine your light bright
You will be received
In love tonight

## 1-8-2024

Between the bees knees
You will see, all there is to be
Nothing and everything
*Buzz, buzz, bizz*
My queen bee, look after me
Believe in what you see
There is no wrong or right
You can hear me in the night
Buzzing in your ears
The new way forward
Without any fears
Know the time is near

*Soon it will be time*
*To decide which way to go*
*Up above or below*

*Are they the same?*
Yes, this was a test
Of discernment
There is no left or right
It is all now
Unity is upon you
This is how to bring it to you

*What if you aren't moving?*
The illustration is that you "move"
But everything else is moving for you
So what are you going to "move" to?
What are you going to invite in?
Farmland or Mansions?
There are no limits to this future

Become gratitude
Move forward
You know what to do
Wake up and say "Hooray" for another day
To play
In this reality

## 1-11-2024

That dark spot is calling me again
I pretend not to see it
Sublime consciousness awaits
If I take the bait
The dark spot in my heart
Awaits eternity
*What fear do you hold?*
It is you who needs to let go
The shadow does not block you
"Make friends with me" it says cheerfully

*Is this temptation to move away?*
*From infinite intelligence*
*Alignment and faith*
*All that is of the creator light?*
Yes, you are right
Don't be misunderstood
Trickery
Is just a perception
Misunderstood
Look under your hood
You will see it is a human condition
That it is not just demons that have needs
There is a misconception
As humans create these "demons"
That trick you

*Moving away from the light*
*That is moving away from*
*Love being understood*

Demons, we pretend they don't exist
And yet they still persist
Being in this world
We all have that potential
Every second
To start our day in a new way
We can give Love or add to Hate
We can pursue joy or trick ourselves
***Where do you want to dwell?***

# 1-31-2024

Crystal bath, erase the past
A New Day is to come
Let all that has been done
*Unwind*
*Erase*
It is time to start the new race
Feet below the earth, create a new birth
Centuries old

A new story is to be told
*Unifying*
*Expanding*
*Understanding*
Drawing with the light
A new breath to shine bright
Just as your mother held you tight
Allow your body to turn to light
Do not be afraid of the unknown
That is only a lower tone
Go forth with might
Let wisdom be your plight (*your promise*)

It's your turn now, start a new day
Before the old grows older
It's time for you to turn your shoulder

*Integrate now*
*Allow*


The one with the night light
You get your wings and take flight
Be on your way, little birds

Your voices have been heard
Your shoulders has been lifted
Yes, you are all gifted
Creator knows your name
This is not a game, this is not a simulator
This is you elevating
Becoming one again with the sun
A child lost, found its way through the field
The light of day

A new order to come
It may be slow, or it may be fast
It depends on your life path
Continue holding hope in your heart
That is your first place to start
Before the dawn of the day
There was a darkness that was laid
You cannot have unity with just one

*Do you carry both? Yes*
Do not let the darkness of your past
Carry you away from your path
There must be balance of both sides in you
You must see the dark as love too
As it's only lower aspects of You

We are here to show you the way
To integrate the night and the day
To hold both as equals

Be free now of your judgments and your shame
There's no one left to blame
Sometimes you may feel insane
Know that is just the game

You must move past the ideas
That were laid down in the past
You must integrate your fate
Knowing that you are never late
Before you, there was one
There was the sun

*Children of the Earth*
With love at the core of who you are
Time for a new star
One that is conscious of the other realms
It's your time, my child, to be found

It's time for your light to be seen
Gleaming
Beaming those rays of light for days
Discovering more of who you are
Beyond these stars
*You came here to transform the old to the new*
*You came here to be the cocoon and the butterfly*
*You came with me to shift the times*
*You came here to make new rhymes*
That shows the way to the new time
To show the way to the new day

The past has been forged
Step up in your courage
Step up, step forward
Towards the highest good
Towards that, which is yours
*Peace*
*Love*
*Joy*

*Take that baby step now*
*We are here to show you how*


**My sweet babies**
As you transform, from old to young
There is a new song that will be sung
In your name, they will praise
The ones who lead the way
For their struggles and their pain
For their courage to go a different way
They will know and understand
That you respected the land
The holy ground beneath your feet
**Dear ones**
You have forgotten how to greet
Trying to be all neat

Hold your way, you know this pain
Is temporary in order to gain
An expanded vision
Of the direction of change

**Sweet ones**
There will be many that say you are insane
Remember to smile and say their name
Help them remember who they are
They are here playing their role as well
Pushing you to overcome
So remember, not to dwell
On those who are unkind
They may be the darkness that needs the light
They are part of you, hidden and unseen
Brought forth
Open that door for unison

Just a hope, a prayer will do
Allow your divine team to take care
Of the rest for you
And sweet ones, as we go
We send you all our love

**///**

Living in your core truth
Is another layer of authenticity
It's who you are beyond your fear
Of the rejection in society
Moving beyond what others think
Moving beyond the layers in the sink
Of draining energy
Set free labels and judgments
For ourselves and everyone else
*This is our ascension*
*This is our path*
To let go of the stories of the past
When we move through that and truly let it go
Nothing else can keep us down and take hold
Because at this stage you will know
You are just pure
*Energy*

Connecting with all that you see
Knowing underneath, it's all You
That is the **TRUTH**
There will be waves of forgetting
There will be ways of knowing
It'll be waves of understanding
Wisdom is a wave
Sometimes you are on the same page

In that flow
And sometimes it's okay to just not know
And understand there is a reason
So you can grow
Lessons are the greatest form
Of wisdom that we know
That push us deeper
Into our own soul's
*Light*

*Be here now*
Enjoy your newfound wisdom
Enjoy the freedom
And remember to be here for every person
Every being—plants, animal and beyond

The waves of Metatron
Are available
Just lie down on the table
And see a New World
It's ancient and it's new
That's what you're here to do
To become and receive
*Yes, my love, that is your destiny*

In the beauty that abounds
Love can be found
Stay on these tracks
And just relax

## 2-1-2024

The birth of the New Day
A diamond
Blue light in flight

*The dragons appear after many years*
*Laying in the land, in our sand*

Planting the seeds we all will need
After the time of darkness
Appears the light
The fire burns bright
For humanity is saved

***It is happening now***
Now that the dragons are awake
Yes, there will be earthquakes
Steady and calm in your heart
This is where you start
To plant your seed for the future
For You and Me
And the "I"
That "sees"
Pure divinity
The essence of the soul
Uncovered

## 2-2-2024

*She is from the amazing race*
*She is the new "You"*
*She will show you what to do*
*She is the awakened one*

A layer of skin around you
Your mother from another galaxy
A womb to set you free
A mother for humanity
That is the healed version
Of divine masculinity
Balancing femininity
Becoming one soul with two
That is an expression of the healed
Version of "You"
Masculine and feminine, together as one
You can then become
The mother and father of all children
The trifecta of all three living fully inside
Heals humanities wounds
Becoming whole again

*The Becoming—it will be called*
*The beautiful unfolding of it all*

**Stand tall, little ones**
Yes, you will have two suns
One above and one below
The sun and moon merge
As one light

*I ask: "What can we do to keep balance*
*through this transformation?*

Rely on your own information
Trust your inner knowing
Test your discernment
Stay in heart, in love frequency
Stay within higher energy
Notice what drains you
Bring in the color blue
From a rainbow of all blue light
Go with the flow of the water deep below
Trust you will not be in harm

Expand your neuro-connectivity
In your brain flow circuitry
Tap into the evolved higher mind
It is available for you at this time
Ask *and* feel *and* know
And it will be real, in your heart

*Heal*

## 2-3-2024

"It is them and not you"
Yes, that is partially true, but you see that the lack in them
Is a reflection of a lack in you—it does relate
Don't make the mistake of not integrating this truth

There is a piece of You walking in the shadow of the underworld
And there is a piece of You in the middle world
In this 3-D reality
And there's a piece of You in the heavens
In the higher dimensions, as you grow into your ascension
Your soul grows in the underworld
Tackling new challenges, new levels of learning
Even if you are "asleep", there is a layer of this happening

Your body is very aware of the changes happening
Both here and there
Since you are conscious and reading this
You can guide the way to a higher state
Yes, you are in control of that part of your fate
And yes, you will reach those gates
Have no fear, as it is just a journey
And for many journeys, there will be mistakes
Along your way
Allow for them to appear
***Do not self-judge***
***But do learn***
You can remember and not judge
Be one now, with all three of You

*Integrate "Them"*
*The I, You, and Me*

Some will go and some will stay
There is no right or wrong way
Just proceed on your path
And take a bath in the beauty that surrounds you

**My dears**
You are all on the right path
You do not have to steer
In your quiet practice you will hear
Which way to go, if you open and allow
**Be not afraid - Be not afraid**
**BE NOT AFRAID**
This is important enough to say, again and again
Time to loosen that plug, that connection
Time to reintegrate into a new dimension
Move your cords to that space, to that plug
You will know more, soon enough
That is all, we send you our love

**///**

Stella frequency is the star within the earth
Stella is the pearl that holds both the moon and sun
Stella is the star within the earths core
Stella is the Unity star
The child of the cosmos
That lives within the Earth
She is about to give birth
Making something beautiful
For the humanity that is ready

Who have been patiently waiting
No longer my friends, the old earth is fading
She will be born bright again
Hold hands together
Hold her energy and pass it on

*Your beauty shines bright in the dark night*
*Above and below, they will reunite*

You will have your birthright
You may travel there tonight
Set your attention for ease and Grace
(The daughter of the new race)
As this is a higher dimensional place
You bring this to the human race

*Stella take your place*
*You are a leader, you have been called*
*You do not have to choose to remain small*

This is your highest path of contribution
***Know it now, know it well***
Connect in with the universal clock
Stay away from TikTok
Time and dimension is just a space
A speck in outer space
Allow us to bring you beyond
Allow us to show you the new time
You will learn how
And you will teach, but not preach
As you must hold one foot here and one foot there
A delicate balance
***Go forward and speak***

Feet energy, gut energy, and head energy
Be in the flow as the magnets are changing
Do not anchor in just one way
In order to play, you must anchor in all three
The birds and the bees
They are your example
They have mastered this
Now it's your turn to experience that bliss
In balance with all there is

Go now, my child, and play with this
This is your day to experiment
To go beyond, and yet, go deeper within
With love as your guide
You will fly high
—*In all directions*

## 2-4-2024

The Mayans will instruct you
A race without a place

*Yes, you are an enlightened seed*
*You came to spread your seed light across eternity*

Burn bright, for all the ones lost in the night
So they may find their way home

***I ask: "What is home for us?"***
A learning place

Where the air tastes of beauty
Different and unique

And all we can speak is
***Pure***
***Ether***

# 2-5-2024

**I**

I am right and I am wrong
It's there that I found my truth in my song
In the tall trees and their roots
A new dawn is coming
The birds and the bees
Sing to me this new sound
A *hum, a hymn*
Cracked open to the knowing
We are light at our core
In our truth center
Becoming our crystalline presence

Be in your truth
Embrace this new face
One of light, one of dark erased
Just purity of spirit persists
This is your gift
To know that you can transcend
Time and space
To assist, lifting the human race

Beautiful ones
Listen in
----*pause*
And you will notice a spin
A spinning sensation
Lifting you to the new nation

This is our ascension
Moving into a new story
One that is young and old

Ready for the glory of the new day
When we all transform, the fear goes away
Suffering no more
*Feel that now!*
Don't worry on how
Just be with that feeling
Coming up from your feet

You all are beautiful angels
Be still now, as it is not far
Coming in spades
To lift us up to the New Day
*Beautiful souls*
You all know the way
Start now
The New Day


**II**

Write a story of the new glory
Here already in the cosmic plane
There is nothing more to gain
By being in the past
The old game is finished at last

You know which way to go
You must let go of control
Allow the bees to carry you
To your Destiny
No more pushing the carriage

*Take a seat for the golden ride*
*You will understand more before you die*

The new age has only just begun
Ionized air
Golden Healer will repair
**Breathe deeper**
A walker
Awake
Between the two worlds
Between the two gates
Above and below
The earth rotates
Spinning, weaving, the Golden Age
Hands on your heart
Your guides will show the way
Be present to this everyday

Practice is what matters
Do nothing but this
It will lead you to your bliss

With a kiss goodbye
We send you on your way
Hold the cosmic heart
Focus on that today
It will keep you awake

Each spirit-body complex, holds a light code

*When we come together in community*
*We lend our codes to create a key*
*That moves us on our path*
*Towards our Destiny*

And most important

It moves Earth towards its highest
Potentiality

This key can heal disease, not alone on the throne
We come together to build a new home
The elders will tell
The story they weave
*Of a golden child*
*This child is the key*
A Temple of Love
For all humanity

## 2-28-2024

Now is the time to turn to the divine
To take a break, to listen within
Your dreams, your wishes
Allow them to come in
Do not mistake, this road you must take

*Dream big, my little friends*
Money is not a means to an end
Truth be told you will grow old
And awaken to your fairy friends

*"A"*
The power in the symbol
Feel the power of *A*, feel the power of *B*
Soon you will see
The power in the words you speak
*It's time to come home, dear ones*
It's time to allow yourself to feel it all
*Be it all*

Know your truth, and you cannot fall
Walk the glass bridge
Over the abyss
With love and trust in your heart
You will glide over to the other side
This may not come for many years
*You all must be patient, my dears*
Do not rush the journey
For now, just be

Allow emotions to roll from thy
Be inspired by the bee

And take a nap in a flower
Nap here for an hour
Receive the nectar that you need
Then go out and seed
Our future collective
Destiny

## 2-29-2024

Beauty awaits at the gates of eternal rest
When you pass the final test
Of saying yes to who you are

*You are a star*
*Underneath that sheet of dust*
*At your feet*
*So rise from the ash of your past*

Start anew and renewed
A journey worth taking
Make no mistake
This is not your fate
But a choice worth making

## 2-29-2024.2

The fullness of me
A light in the dark
Has come together
Created a spark
Of full acceptance
No longer one or the other
With the balance of the two together
Now there's just one
Powered by the sun and moon
The two in one makes three
Unity, of the Holy Trinity

This is revelations
For the days to come
This is the time to make change
Towards a better way
Towards your hearts desire
To light up your fire

I am a seed frequency
I plant your seed
In multidimensionality
So you may grow
And sow into manifestation
Of your higher self

*Awakening the codes of light*
*Along your path*
*So you may walk more clearly*
*Birthing your dream*
*Into this creative, giving planet*

I am a birthing queen
*Queen bee*
I take care of my children's seeds
And help them grow
It's more than birthing though
It's support along the way
It's holding your hand as you graduate
And then letting you go
Being free, standing tall
Love the breeze that blows you
And sets you free along your path
Of greatness, of the inner you
That knows and lives in your truth

There will be a day that comes
When the manifestation is done
When there are no longer any seeds to sow
Until then we hold each other's hand as we grow
We must, for a seed is hard to grow
*All alone*
We grow more when we have community
When we have a loving, caring tribe
Right at our side

You know how to grow
Some of it will be easy, some of it not
As we step into the light
There will be those challenges
Look to your left and your right
To see who stands beside you
*Who do you want to carry you?*

Surround yourself with a loving team
Surround yourself with your heart light

Shining ever so bright
Yes, you are a light guiding the way
For others who shall come with you soon
Yes, you remain at noon
It is easier now
The surrender helps show you how
By letting go, the taller you can grow
Being free of limitations
Being free from all nations
Remembering you are clay
Of the source, of the earths core

*How do you want to mold yourself?*
*How are you molding your life?*

**Bright little angels**
As you are both the Earth and the light
Traveling within your own universe
Your body holds this inside
So you never die
You can explore all there is
***And so much more***

Goodnight, my child
Good morning to the new light
You have done all right
***And so much more***
***And so much more***

Close your eyes, open the door
The New Earth awaits you
Walk into her core
Let the beauty surround you
Unbound you

All the chords
Of suffering, of pain
Feeling that there is nothing to gain
That you are doing it all wrong
This time, it's time to let it go
It's time for you to know
How much more there is
How much more in the unseen
In the bliss of source's arms
You can do no harm
Your job is to remember
Remember why you are here
And to walk your path with no fear

*In full confidence*
*In the fullness of who you are*
*And those who know you will see you*
*My little star*

You are a present to the universe
You have lifted all the curses
***You have walked the dark path***
***You have walked the light path***
***You have walked the middle earth***

You have carried the weight
Of the collective
The collective consciousness
Has been cleared
***You have changed, my dear***
Gently walk your path
With love at your back
We surround you now
You know, this is how

To proceed
With integrity
You are the bees knees
Creating portals, creating joy
Innocence and beauty
Behind the mask
Lies this truth
The blessedness of You

Free yourself
Unplug the last cord
*Of your discord*
*Of the enduring*
*Of the pain of others*

Go and be a mother
Connect into that consciousness
Out of the collective and into the higher layer
Connect your consciousness and plug
Into the network of the 5th Dimension
It is now time for Ascension
The work is complete
You have it all at your feet
*Float softly, my dear*
*Float, your time is near*
Connect your heart vibrations
Into the New Earth consciousness
Feel the lift, this is a gift
Moving into the fifth
This is your time to decide
*Ride or die*
*Ride or fly*
*Or reside in both*

It's here for you to decide
The door of light awaits
They welcome you through those gates

*I know in my heart*
*I am here to bring in this new consciousness*
*And plug it into the collective*
*To create portals of Ascension*

This is my direction
With love as my guide
I will ride and fly
Those that are ready
No longer needing to hide
I can now fly
Freely without harm
I can disarm the old paradigm
To create a new time and story
With love, in our glory
Of a rising
Human consciousness

## 3-3-2024

You have opened up a new door
To the New Earth gates
The balance of earth now awaits
Your arrival

The codes to the old program
Have been broken
You have woken
The dormant mind
Into the new space and the new time
To explore more

*Yes, my dear ones*
Yes, with excitement in your hearts
This is the spark that you need to be free
To be one with the breeze
Know thy name, as it will keep you sane
Know thy name and free yourself from this game
Of limitation, of segregation
Of being one with one nation

It is time to awaken
It is time for you to know
And it's time for you to show
How your Ascension looks like in action

Breathe in the new air
Calibrate the new water in you
And your hair strands
So you are one with it all
You are just a ball of energy
Of light

You must evolve and it is your right
We come on strongly now
More so than in the past
It is time now for you to understand
To let go of all that holds you back

Take up the sword of light
That holds more than you know
Step out of time
Step into the divine
Be one with your land
The time is at the hand
The hand that takes the sword
The hand that takes the action forward

*Break free, break free*
From your own chains around your feet
*Break free, break free, little bee*
And buzz around and you will see

*The golden child, the golden light*
*The golden child whose birth is tonight*
*Each one of you, birthed anew*

On some level, you know it's true
*You are ready*
Hear me clearly
*You ARE ready*

In your heart, this love sparks
These words provoke
Yes, that's how they were spoke
With vigor, with conviction
But most of all, with love

Walk that glass bridge
From the cave that you've been hiding in
To the cliff high above
*What is an illusion?*
*What is real?*
That is for you to feel
Feel the feet, feel the glass beneath
*Breaking*
And know
Even in the flight of falling
You find your wings

You can never die
You are just reborn inside
Rebirth is an inside job
Burn the ashes of the pain
Burn all that you have not gained
Burn the programs that hold you back
With the Serafin flame
Your "will" to gain
The joy of being human

If discernment compounds you
*Learn your truth*
If your vision is unclear
*Use the flame to burn away the fog*
If your feet are not grounded
*Within the soul of yourself*
*Make room and call it back*

No, you are not under attack
It may seem like that
This is strange and new
And out of the blue

But it has to be to expand you
Into the beauty and the life of your light

*No matter who I have been*
*I know who I am*
*Love*

Transforming time and space
Bringing us to a new place
Being part of the new birth

Love and guidance are on its way
To help you navigate the new
Be here now and trust and honor
**Be here, my friend, it is our honor**
**To help you**
Through the Wake of your times
With these rhymes
Let us help you navigate
Through the darkness
The ending taking place
The systems crashing
It is time to take your place
Among those that have a lead before
Opening up a new door
To community
To knowing that we need each other
Despite our differences

**Beautiful beings of light**
It is in your right
To spread love across the world
It is time to unfurl
The pedals that you have been given

That have been in the waiting
To blossom, to bloom, to stretch
To find room within this new energy

**Do not wait, do not wait**
For your hand is on the gate
The time has come
You have already won the path ahead
Some of you are already "dead"
Some of you live on
Those who read these words
Are wisdom keepers of the New Earth
They were given to you at birth

*Remember now, remember*
*Feel the remembrance*
*Feel your ancientness*

Your strength is needed
The warrior path is at your back
Do you accept this
Or do you just want to create
More lack?

ME:
***What does it mean to be a warrior on this path?***
It means stepping up at last
Standing tall, even though you may be small
It means leading the changes to the new way
Showing people a new path
To discover more of who they are
And who they've been
— — You are able to time bend
— So go slow, be still

— — Start to feel the vibrations of what you see
— See the vibrations between you and me
— — Feel the vibrations of these words

*Are you in balance?*
*What have you heard?*
Your surroundings matter
*What do you surround yourself with?*
— It can be as simple as a kiss
— — On a cheek
— But when you slow down and really feel that touch
— — The gentle, peaceful, quality of that action
And bring more of that into your day
Bring more of that in a new way
Through play and discovery

## 3-5-2024

Time upside down
So is this city, so is this town
**Which way do we go?**
No one really knows
Topsy turning, around we go
The sun
If I close my eyes and never come back
I will be happy at least to fly again

The time is noon
Time to play another tune
With the sun by my side
I allow the last of "Me"
To be set in the breeze
To join the choir and sing a song
Of a dream released
From the days past
It knows it's time has come
To past

*Allow the disease to take flight*
*Do not put up a fight*
*Release the need to be right*

The song you sing, brings in the beginning
Of a new day realized

## 3-11-2024

The New World is blooming and birthing below our feet
It is the inner sun gaining power, burning and pushing
Everything to the surface

Slowly, we will start to see signs of the New Earth
From this expansion of birth within

But first, the old must go
A new road paved in gold
So first, that which is no longer needed, is being pushed out
*Thoughts of doubt, thoughts of loss, thoughts at any cost*

*It's time to breathe a new breath*
*It is time to rest*

You have all passed another human test
You are on your way to experiencing the new day, in a new way
Moving through the old shadows that haunt you

*Rest dear, and be not in fear*
It's all that needs to surface, to be cleared

Hold true, in trust and faith
This will align you with the new race
That has no face in fear or lower dimensions that are near

Walk the path of the new light aligned, true and bright

Align with the light that shines within
That is your unity consciousness

Embracing in love, the light and the dark

Embracing it all with love
So healing can come through from above
You know your way, there is help coming
But it is your work to do, not ours, in this hour
It's your journey
**Which road will you choose, the old or the new?**

*Be calm, my friends*
*Create the peace within*
*It will mirror back to you in life*
*And in all that you do*

**What energies do you want surrounding you?**
Call those in now

Find the love that sparks within
That is the creator's perception of this dream

Yes, the New World is unseen by some of you
Yet you have the power to dream it true
**Dear ones,**
Your time has come to rise to the skies
Of ultimate potential in love and light
**Go now, take flight**
**Go now, and be free**
**Go now, you will see**
The words I speak
Are here at your feet
Ready to be grounded within

*This is your calling and so it begins*

So the time has come of the double sun
Of the New Earth

This is the day of her birth
You will start to see two suns in the sky
Representing Me and I
With You and Me and I
Unity of the three
Combined
Sing low, sing high
Your feet will know
Where to go

*Stand tall, my friend*
You will not fall
For today is the day of truth for all
That love is already here
That love has conquered fear
The truth has come
It cannot be undone
This day they'll sing
*PRAISE*
We made it
Beyond all odds
No fear or cause
Could take this dream away

Thank you, thank you for being part of this
It is now time to walk into your bliss
Into the abyss that is just pure love

Now, my friends, be one
Together, be free
To Rome (**roam**)
And play
With your conscious day
Love is here to stay

*Rise above the fog*
*Rise to the double sun*
*Rise to clarity*
*Rise to the light*

And let your heart shine bright
Day and night
Love lasts, my friends
Love together, never ends

# 3-17-2024

Trust in yourself, see the truth
Beyond the gates, there lies your fate
With love as your knowing
You keep on growing
Love by your side
We need for you to rise
Be the change you seek
It is not for the weak
It takes courage to be who you came to be

Yes, you need your sleep
The pain you feel will help you heal
So be with it and know it will have it it's time to go

## 4-8-2024

Light arise
From the solar skies
Set us free
From all disease
Allow the new to come
The birth has begun

*For the love of all creatures*
*For the love in all time and space*
*Now is the time for the new race*

They will arrive in due time
They will emerge from the divine
They will lead the way, to the new day
To the fall and the rise
They will not be disguised
They will show their face
To the new human race

Be strong, be silent
During the birth
Go inwards to feel the vibration rising
Yes, afterwards, there will be new "timing"
The shift will be felt and seen
By those in the new energies
Be the love, my friends

This story is only just begun

**4-9-2024**

You have opened a new door
To explore your inner working
You have not been here before
The new You to explore
The new year, we cannot see
It's a past eternity

*This is the second coming of Christ light*

It happened during the darkest of the night
In daylight get ready to take flight
To the New Earth
She is here, she is birthed
***Feel it in the sun rays***
***Feel it in the morning of the new day***
***Feel it as you look at the spring dew***
And feel brand new
The sparkle of Stargrass
Reminds you of your past
Reminds you of the vastness
Of the spark that you are
***Little star***
You are on your way
Shine brightly in this new day
***Have no fear***
That is old energy and the new is here
The new is filled with hope
The new is filled with love yet to come
The new day blooms a new flower
In this very hour
Align your heart energy
With this song

It's vibrancy is so strong
Being one with the hour
Let go of the towers
That tumble as the Phoenix rises
A new foundation made with its ash

New fertile soil for your wishes
Letting go of the past
Plant the new seed that will last
In this new creation
In this new planet energy

**Be here now, my friends**
The door has been unlocked

*Stop watching the clock*
*Start watching the sun*
*She will show you the way*

Between the light and the day
And open up the doors of your heart
In a whole new way

Be free as the bees
Humming and buzzing their frequency
**Surrender**
**And let love take its course**

## 4-11-2024

I am the One
The unknown
The One with one thousand wings
Hear me sing
I tone for you all that is true
In beauty and grace
For the entire human race

*Be free, my little bees*
From the constraints around your knees
With love by your side
It is this I abide
To clear and free you from all disease

*Bring you to your knees*
*(watch your little seeds)*

You will know which way to go
Surrender now, all that you have
To be blessed with all that there is
That exists in your one wish
For the world to know
All the love
It holds

## 4-19-2024

Love is the only way to the new day
Open the door to explore the new way
In a new way to live life
Know all is okay

*Gold and water blue*
*Into the lake with you*
*Bathe in the sparkling light*
*And sleep well tonight*

**Just rest**
Golden egg, laid within
Is the reflection of the dream you are in

**Beautiful ladies**
You create the new race
Of roses and emeralds laid
At the feet of the new king
Bring peace to Earth
With this new birth
Of a new reality yet to be seen
No, it's is not just a dream
But a reality yet to be heard
Be the one, friend and foe
Each of you know which way to go
Towards Light and Love
Get out of your head
Hold your hands
To your heart
*Feel* a new start

## 4-24-2024

Divine Rome
In the DaVinci code
Stolen from me
There is a key in the secret geometry
*1, 2, 2, 9*
It's the beginning and end of time
A door, a gate
Open and closed
But it's not too late
Reopen and explore

*There is so much more*
*Than what is seen and what is known*
*How far are you willing to go?*

Below the surface
Into a cave you know
An elevator through time and space
To the surface, they rise to see the sun
Then you will know humanity has won

The golden shield will fall
And it will tell all
The truth that you seek
Remains under your feet

A New Earth, a new race is underway
The time is now, right now, today
Make the most of it
As the shield will come down
Those not ready may drown in sorrow
That they won't have a tomorrow

They will need to find new ways to behave
An eye for an eye is the old way

*What will your next level soul be?*

They come running to tell you
To listen and you will receive
They are the masters you seek
**Allow them in**
Open your doors to them
The divine mothers of humanity
Knowledge seekers, wisdom keepers
Young and old
Find a new way to grow

## 4-27-2024

What if we use math (*sacred geometry*)
To unify the dark in light?
Unifold the numbers into shapes
Light Language is the flow
Of numbers in space
Forming new geometries

*I ask:*
*"Could Light Language drawings elevate the soul?"*

Yes, indeed that is to unfold
Take your soul song and form it into geometry
To access higher dimensional learnings
And wisdom of evolution
That is the "solution"

You can't have geometry without the negative space
To form something sacred, you must have dark and light
Combined
There is a quality of beauty in darkness we have forgotten
In this reality, we need both

*Without darkness*
*There is only a blank canvas*

## 4-27-2024.2

You must go now and be
Sing your song to them
And change the reality dream
Griding the trees around me
Angry Birds must fly away
The new Sun is coming
Calvary will lead the way
Down a new path unknown

The sun is rising above the horizon
There is two rivers I walk
Two heart beats
The baby is in me
She is inside you now

*You will see*
*She is the one speaking*

Plant the nectar, plant the seed
A midnight, summer dream
That is where she will be seen
As the crow flies wide
In a baron land of tears
You have known each other for years

*Between the bee's knees*
*Knowing the forest from the trees*
*Listen to Horus speak*
*And you will be set free*

A single swan in the lake
Holds the wisdom of holy water

Tangled, holds no more
Allow your heart to open
To Grace, see the Lady's face
Allow swan energy to mix with mine

*Beyond space and time*
*The beauty of the now*
*Has arrived and will still be*

Be still, let go of your will
Allow angels to speak
Through pen and paper
Here she lays her eggs
And a new chapter
For a new time
Beyond words and rhythm
In the stillness
Of just
Being

## 4-29-2024

As above, as below
As a new day blooms
Hear my song I sing to you

One eye in heaven, and one in earth
Two, to witness the new birth

I am the portal and the key
That will set you free
With humility

This is Lady Grace
A beginning of the new race
I sing for the small and the tall
Every being, large or small
This is a new day!
***Rejoice!***

The light that comes
From burning the old
Is as beautiful as a rose
Burning letters and stories
Of the past can lead to
New glory, a new story
More brilliant and built to last

Do I need to choose between which family
To live with the ancestor line or the one with divine?
Can the bee and the mouse live in the same house?

*Yes, both worlds exist*

Perhaps the combining of the two
Not to live separately
But come all together
It will be letting go of demons of the past
You are free to create and live with truth

It has been delivered
You have woke into a new dream
**All is well, my queen**
A bed of yellow roses awaits

## 5-11-2024

They will know your name

*Who resides in you?*
*Is it really You?*
The dragon plays the game
Your world is not the same as it used to be

*Will they know your name?*
*Who will you blame?*
*Are you going insane?*
*Who is speaking now?*
*Is it the devil or ego?*
*Or is it the eagle?*

Discernment is the game
Know it well
Time always tells

*Right from wrong, is it gone?*
*Is this the new song?*

Be in your power
Be mighty
Own your song, play it strong
This is not a game
Don't throw it all away
You are not insane
Know that, always

*Don't allow the shadows of the devil*
*That once was, destroy the new You*

Bare feet, walk on new ground
Step into the Golden Sun
Child, you have won
From old, comes new
The diamond inside of you
Grows in this warming light

Rest now, know you are secure
Held in divine mother hands
To voyage to new lands
The time is the present moment
***Live it - Be it - Enjoy it***
Grinning ear to ear, your baby is here
Have the vision
And allow source to do the rest

## 6-1-2024

There is a new you waiting around the bend
Do not pretend
You will know which way to go
Connect

*Be one with your soul*
*She will know the way, but you must not stay*
*The same*
*In your old ways*

The doors are open to a new way of being
***This will set you free***
***My little honey bees***
An hour, a minute, what is time?
Place your bet on a dime
Crackling through this dimension is a new You
Find your truth in all that you do
Be the change, the currency of the new
Plane of Truth
Becoming the new you
It's in the stars
It is not far, so embrace who you are
***A leader of the new race***

You will find your pace
In the beauty of the healing
Colliding all of "You" into your truth
Set the scene for more to be seen
Spread your wings and sing

***"I am alive!"***

*And smile as you fly*
*Into your new awakening*

No fear, only the essence of you, my dears
Be the change you seek

**Little bee**
Drops of honey at your feet
Light up all that you need
***To succeed***
***Sweet victory!***

## 6-21-2024

Leaps and bounds
Allow the new to be found
In the sky above
In the Earth below
This is where we must go

*To reconnect with your truest essence*
*To know that you are a present*
*For the world*

***You... are... loved... dearly***
No need to fear
Whether partner is close or near
You are a partner to yourself
And the divine
It is time to shine your light
Brightly

## 6-21-2024

*The tears stuck in my third eye*
*That wanted to flow*
*And was not allowed*
*The tears stuck in my soul*

It's time to let those roll
To the mother of the sea
To divinity
To turn into waves
That push me forward
To show up in a new way

Take me home
To my soul unknown
The parts of me
That still need to be explored

**Who am I?**

## 6-27-2024

We are all saviors if we want to be
We all have the power to change this world
To lift the demons away
Each one of us, today
Can choose to shift the energy
To the new

Be the spiritual warrior
You are enough
Be in your trust
And let love guide the way

**7-1-2024**
JULY FLAMES

Burn away the thoughts of not being good enough
*You are here, are you not?*
Good enough to be chosen for this journey
To a world called Gaia
I'm not going to lie, it will be a busy July
The flames will rise high

Take care of your feet
Grounded for the lightning's beat
Be prepared for a crackle in the air
Whether it be fair or unfair

*Your heart still beats*
*Do not feel defeat*

You never know who you will meet
Allow the wind to blow your hair
In the open space
Where destruction took place
And now it is the opening, a gateway of the divine
You will get through it safe
And integrate your old and new
Look for it
In everything you say and do
Think and feel
You are the new
***Becoming real***

## 7-2-2024

In the land of make believe
I see you standing there
Take a step in
This is not a dare
But you will fall into the unknown
There is fear
As the program does not want you here

*Know what you want*
*Hold that and jump*

The tunnel of light
Will be created
A wish
A opening
To explore more
The land of make believe is at your feet

*"Will you take the lead?"*
*Yes*

This is your land, my friend
This is where you can fly free
So come on in and join me
A place of fun and play
To be here all day
This is not a chore
This is somewhere you adore
A land that is truly just yours

*Be in love*
*In the make believe*

Soon you will see
This reality is not an illusion
Rid yourself of the confusion
Journey with me!
This is your destiny

*Love has no end or beginning*
*This land of love, will be forever yours*

So open that door and allow
You will know how
We bow to you for all that you do
As you send yourself in and open
***Allow***
Your inner knowing to show you how
***Allow***
It is freeing
You need no reason to shut this out
***Allow***
Us to lead you through
***The fray***

Join us
To see your imagination unexplored
Dream now
Fully awake

## 7-5-2024

The land of make believe is more real
Than your reality

*What happens if you don't believe?*
You'll never get to see
The miracles that occur
Life will be just a blur

*Come home now*
Don't delay, for today is your day
To welcome all your friends
From Neverland

*Ride the final wave*
Be with us, come and play
Leave some of your responsibilities
Behind, be in the joy of the now

*Take a chance*
Fall in love with a new romance
Take a leap of faith
The land of make-believe
Is just a thought away

*We love you, always*

## 7-14-2024

The mountain is where I need to be
The mountain will set you free
From all of the musts and have too's

*Like the night bee*
*Who sleeps peacefully*
*No worries in its head*

Relax and trust every now moment that creates the next
Go back to bed and awake again renewed
Relax, we got your back, and your future too
Be here now and you'll know what to do
Those you adore, will come to you
If you are clear and true

*Be your own best friend, my dear*
*Find the joy of being here*

"The order of beauty"
***What does this mean?***

You heard it in a dream
Upon walking in remembrance
Of what once was omnipresence
A world far away, yet close to your heart

A New World you start
One where beauty lead leads the way
A universal law, in fact
Where beauty is acknowledged
Where it blooms in every microcosm
Beauty in every breath

Get out of your head and create this now place
This is what you came to create
***So go and make!***

You are the leader of this game
***Take the reins***

## 7-17-2024

TULU planet of marble blue
Orange color face from space
Time capsule opened
Emerges the great race

Yellow and blue diamond
Expand into my field
Through my sacred work
Bring the flames to the blessed tree
Mount Shasta has a gift for me
Telo-tulu, the balance of the two
Gold and the blue
Activated in sacred flames

*No, not a game*
*This is the work you came to do*
*The journey to find the real you*

Your gifts unleashed
Father time is released
Joy will come to you
***You draw it in, slow down, take it all in***
The peace you seek, the harmony you feel

All will be well
You have broke the spell

## 7-26-2024

August energies we explore
There is so much to do in this new season
Birds and bees, giving us their song
Follow the lead, hum a song of joy
It's time to explore the new energy
*Rejoice!*
Get up off your seat, come dance with me
In the warm summer breeze, we explore
It's time for you to see the magic
That is always here
To turn the gloom and doom
Into a new moon phase
To take the reins of light
See the other side of night
*Go explore*
*What if we all decided to open that door?*
If we greet everyone from the love of our core
If we could walk with authentic foundation
*This is me,* I want to be seen
I am wounded, but not today
Today I am pure

*Is it scary to be wide open like that?*
*Are you afraid of an attack?*
It's time to explore, to uncover, to reveal
The shadows still lingering, lurking
Time to start living the dream
Wide and awake
Not afraid of making mistakes
So go for it
A new tide awaits your shore
*We adore you*

**7-30-2024**

It's time to explore a new open door
To make friends with fear

To open your light
To let in the fear, *feel it*
And know that it will lead
You to see the darkest part
Of thee

You fear the dark
That is where you start
When you can see the dark
And come out the other side
That is winning
You then know
*And knowing is power*

The crows know the dark
That is where they live
That is their gift
Living in the underworld
Has shown them
The power and abilities to shapeshift
The matrix

*There is light in the air*
Breathe it in
Let go of fear

## 9-1-2024

Soul star magic
Not far from turbulent times
Practice: stay within your energy
Empowerment and prayer
Remember, Love is always here
Change in the weather, change in the time
Brings new energy to the paradigm
Stay your course and don't be swayed
To another way
Align to your truth is always the way
Be here in your heart, shining light
Be a new spark of energy
That will light the way
During the darkest days

Remember your goal, your dream
Of new light being streamed

An explosion of Love compelling you
To enter the New Earth
This is the focus to hold
No matter what is being told
*Awake and create!*

*Dear creators,*
Shine your light that is the divine
Shine bright for others to see
And shift humanity into the New Earth energy
*Birth*

## 10-4-2024

Forget the thoughts of yesterday
And follow the breeze
She will lead
To new opportunities
And as the sun rises
Be aware there are some surprises
Follow your own inner guidance
**Believe**

You do not have to fight over love or time
Or a reason to be

*Drop everything and follow your destiny*

**Yes, we are ready for the portal**
**We are ready for the quickening**
**We are ready for the anger to rise**
Into the burning night sky
With fierce truth in our heart
The warrior must start
The fire of destruction and rebirth

This must happen to create the move
Of humanity to the New Earth

The battles to come, my dear ones
You must fight for love and light
So take this seed of fire and use it well
As you may be walking through
Your own personal hell

*Purge this earth of unrighteous anger*

Purge the consciousness of the collective
The fire has returned and we must use it well
The fire has returned because of the dry well
The thirst of spiritual knowledge must come first

Quantum timeline entanglement
Is coming undone
***Listen to your Sun***
The ultimate fire that shines bright
And know that you don't have to be right
***Just listen***

The time of reckoning has begun
So dream girl, dream
Of the rising Sun
On a new horizon
Beyond the fire
Walk in it, walk-through it
***Purify***

189

# *the*
# CLOSING

189

## A NEW TIME HAS ARRIVED

*Spirit is always by your side*

I don't know what is to come. Friends, all I know is this is not the end. This year has arrived with new energies, yet there is so much surfacing.

Many of you are struggling. For many, it is walking into this year with more fear than the year before. For others, it is an astronomical financial struggle, and for some, it's both and more.

I don't have the answers. I don't have a magic wand that can make it all change. I am also in this game.

*So why am I writing all of this?*

Because deep down, I know and believe we will be shown a new road to take, to travel on—that we are not helpless—that now is the time for a new start, and it starts with your heart.

It's to go within and know. To have the wisdom to know which way to go, to know when or what to surrender. Anything that is spiking fear, look into it as a clear mirror. Is it taking you out of your power or energizing you to stand taller?

My friend, the shift has arrived. Stand tall, no matter what arises. Stand tall to the forces that want you small, that want you powerless, that want you separated.

You may have heard there is a frequency war. What does that mean? We won't be slaves anymore to someone else's dream. What is enslaving you now? It's time to break free from the chains that bind us. It's time to step deeper into trust.

Right now, it's about maintaining our frequency—to raise each other up, to continue to be AWARE (conscious, awake, awakened) of what is happening. As it is wanting us in survival mode or causing fear and stress.

*Rise above it. Do not fear it.*

*"How?"*
That is what we are here to learn. I can't tell you how. I am not certain myself, but what I can tell you is what my truth is leading me to.

Wake up every day renewed. It is waking into a new dream. It is retaining hope. It is knowing that my magic wand is the spark in my heart, my light, my purpose. That I am not going to give up on my purpose. That I am going to lead my day—realigning my energy to positive intentions, to will my energy to create a different outcome, to take the driver's seat on my frequency, to empower myself and rise above the circumstances.

***Will you end the day and still have debt or illness?***
Perhaps, yes.

***Then what will have changed?***
The knowledge that you gained. The self-esteem and

confidence—knowing that you pursued your dream. That you have pushed the needle closer. That you have gained the courage to reject the machine. That you gave it your all. That you stood tall in your truth and energy. That you did not self-sabotage. That you did not fall victim. And you know you are one step closer to your desired future.

*Do not give up on you.*

We need you. I believe in you because I believe in myself. We are all linked. It's time to rise together. It's time to come together as forces try to take our energy down.

*It's time for me to accept and forgive that which has led me to my current circumstances, which means forgiving myself.*

I know each day I have a choice, and I can take responsibility for the choices I make. Otherwise, I choose to be a victim, feel helpless. When I forgive myself, I take responsibility, and I can help make each day a little bit Brighter than the last.

*Affirmation:*
*I rise above that which is happening to me, as I am aware that it is not me. I am the light of Source and I choose to shine, to be a Sun of the Divine and love where I am at for the growth—and not feel attacked. I am the light of the Sun, the Divine light, and I do not fear or lack.*

I may feel under attack, but the battle is within. It's time to stop battling with yourself. Allow a new birth of truth to be to you. Sit in your peace and grace of energy, and allow peace to conquer the inner beast. Settle the fights.

*Where are you battling?*
*Where are you battling with others or within?*
Allow peace to be your sword and your shield, and see what it will yield.

This is my gift to you—to give yourself these moments of introspection, to reflect. How do these words feel to you? Notice the sensation. What arises inside? What you consume affects you. Can you get out of your head and feel?

Decide what you're watching or reading, and what reaction your body has on you're thoughts, your feelings.

*Then decide to make a change.*

Can you take one thing and change it for the betterment of humanity? Maybe you can't do it for yourself. Frame it differently, as if you're doing it for everyone else.

*I affirm:*
*I commit to notice my frequency and change it for myself, my family, and for humankind.*

*Step in. Step up. You know you are love.*
*Shine that love, my friends.*

I send you blessings and love and support from above. Moving forward each day with love, I pray, knowing each day is a blessing of a new opportunity to step into a higher frequency.

## LETTERS FROM THE STARS

We know who they are
Beings of light from far away
We do not need to know their names
They are our guides
From the big blue sky
Bringing us words on a plate
Filling us with home
That lights the way
To ourselves
***Remembered***

We do not need to know their names
The ones who fills these pages full of words
Of worlds to come
For the old to be undone
To go back to the beginning
And yet, know there is no ending
It is just what it is
***I am, that I am***

To know yourself
Beyond time and space
To be the leaders of the new race
Of humans
That is why we write these letters
And bring these codes
Between the space
Between the "letters"

*A rhyme in time*
*Encoded prose*

*With light codes*
*And hidden secrets*
*Of the rose*

**We love you worlds away**
**We love you every day**
**We love you**

We know you are on your way
To becoming
The best that you can be

So sing loud my friends
Sing your song, bright and true
*May these letters sing to you*
*May they fill your heart with peace*
*May they give you some ease*
A bright new day is on its way
You are a piece of the peace
Of the New World
**Coming**

*LOVE,*
*the Stars*

## PS: A NOTE TO MARY

We love you this much, my dear
To write a whole book for you
So you can sing your song, bright and true
And feel the love beneath your wings
As we lift you up to your dream
*Becoming real*

So we close with this
May we be on your wish list
To create more with you
So together can make all of our dreams come true

*To travel from here to there*
*Time to let down your hair*
*Allow us in the driver seat*
*To enjoy the ride along the way*
*Into the new day*

**///**

To ascend my friend
To expand into your greatness
And love who you are

*Be free little stars*
Galaxies away
We are shining light to you of the new day

*Remember*
Love is not light years away
It shines from your heart today

# DEDICATION

This book series is dedicated to the winged ones:
Thoth, Horus, Isis, Thunderbirds and ASTRID, who are 15th dimensional
blue diamond light beings that have allowed me to access their channel of
consciousness. I am eternally grateful for all spirits that helped contribute
—both known and unknown.

# ACKNOWLEDGMENTS

I am grateful for Cindy Quick, who is always encouraging me to work
with both Astrid and Thoth, lovingly known as "the boys". Cindy's gentle
listening and guidance has propelled me through difficult times, always
shining her light so I can remember mine. Her loving Ariel: the Harmonic
Egg, helped regulated my nervous system which then has moved me
forward in the direction of my destiny and writing this book. Thank you for
your loving support and being a sister for many lifetimes.

~

To my fairy friends Carrie and Sabrina,
thank you for always encouraging me and loving me as I am.

~

To my father, William and Grandma Gokey, guides beyond the veil,
for always being by my side.

~

To my daughter Amaya, love you beyond love.

~

To my hybrid daughter Grace.
I am always and forever with you in the New Earth.

*volume 2*

# SCRIBE FOR THE SKY

*launching fall 2026*

If you have enjoyed this book, look for volume two:
*Scribe for the Sky*

 The author invites you to join her email newsletter, where you can get updates of launches and insights from this work of channeled prose and poetry:
*www.ladybirdpublishing.com*

 If you wish for more in-depth insights of the poems and recorded audio of the author speaking them, please join her *Substack* account:
*https://maryladybird.substack.com*

 You can find Mary Ladybird Spiritlight on *YouTube* channeling Astrid and Light language:
*www.youtube.com/@ladybirdspiritlight*

 If you' want to have a session with the author for a Light language channel session, you may book here for an appointment:
*www.maryladybird.com/spiritlight*

*about the*
## AUTHOR & CHANNELER


Mary Ladybird Spiritlight is a spiritual teacher, channeler, and guide for those navigating the ascension journey. With a deep connection to ancient wisdom and higher-dimensional energies, she brings forth messages of transformation and awakening for the New Earth as well as personal transformation.

*Studies, Certifications & Teachers*
— IFSG Red Ribbon Feng Shui Professional
— American Academy of Metaphysics:
  Feng Shui Professional Program
— Mindful Design Feng Shui School of NYC
— London School of Feng Shui
— Holy Fire Reiki, Level 2
— Crystal Reiki Master
— Pro Crystal Healer
— Melchizedek Method, Level 2
— Shaman Studies with Mary Ann Robbat
— Modern Mystery School, Boston

Mary lives in the US East coast and dreams of van life with her dog and 2 cats. She has a daughter, Amaya, who she hopes will find magic while pursuing the world of science and psychology.

www.ingramcontent.com/pod-product-compliance
Lightning Source LLC
Chambersburg PA
CBHW031039160726
47991CB00005B/1952